LARGER THAN LIFE
EDDIE LARGE

LARGER THAN LIFE
EDDIE LARGE

EDDIE LARGE
WITH
STAFFORD HILDRED

JOHN BLAKE

Published by John Blake Publishing Ltd,
3, Bramber Court, 2 Bramber Road,
London W14 9PB, England

www.blake.co.uk

First published in hardback in 2005

ISBN 1 84454 128 2

British Library Cataloguing-in-Publication Data:

A catalogue record for this book is available from the British Library.

Design by www.envydesign.co.uk

Printed in Great Britain by Creative Print & Design (Wales)

1 3 5 7 9 10 8 6 4 2

Papers used by John Blake Publishing are natural, recyclable products
made from wood grown in sustainable forests. The manufacturing
processes conform to the environmental regulations of the country of
origin.

Every attempt has been made to contact the relevant copyright-holders,
but some were unobtainable. We would be grateful if the appropriate
people could contact us.

Eddie Large: This is for my wife Patsy, my son Ryan, daughters Alison and Samantha, granddaughters Kate Lily and Holly Erin, grandson Nathaniel Edward, Peter H and Chris S, brother Brian and family, sister Irene and family, Dave and Derek, Roy, Janet and Jessica, Kevin and Jean, Kiddo and Margaret, Jean and John, Peter and Joan, Norman and Lucy, Mel and Adrian, Bernard, the Boys of Norbrook, the Boys of B@C, Mr Musker, Mr Shatwell, Papworth people, Mr Jenkins, Jayan, Mr Large, Mandy and Stu, supporters and staff of Manchester City FC, Dolly and George, Teddy and Jessie. Thank you all for standing by me in my several hours of need.

Stafford Hildred: I dedicate this to my wife Janet, daughters Claire and Rebecca and to Tim Ewbank, with whose help and collaboration it was written.

Contents

Introduction

'**Y**ou'd better hurry up, your dad's dying.'
Sometimes it's impossible to take things seriously.
One of the many peculiar problems associated with
being a comedian is that even when critically ill you're
inclined to try to crack jokes instead of doing as you're
told. My worst moments are a bit of a blur to me now,
the memory a confused mixture of fear and humour. A
bit like my life, really. To me it seems like a film.

It started in the middle of the night of Friday, 22
February 2002. I got out of bed to go to the loo. It's an
age thing, I suppose. Next thing I knew I had fainted
and fallen flat out in the bathroom.

The noise woke my wife, Patsy, who asked anxiously,
'What's wrong?'

'I tripped,' I said, trying to think on my feet even if I
felt uncertain about standing on them.

'Why didn't you put the light on?' asked a sleepy Patsy.

'I didn't want to wake you,' I replied, without noticing the irony of the remark.

I was lying, I'm afraid. I was already suffering from very serious heart failure and, in order to get my weight down, the hospital had put me on a very high dose of water tablets and restricted me to a litre of liquid a day. My kidneys were working overtime expelling liquid but I had so little left in my body that they were starting to fail.

I had been feeling very light-headed during the day but didn't say anything to Patsy because I didn't want to worry her. It's a man thing. The following day I presented prizes at a pal's golf club near Taunton and in the evening went to a Variety Club awards ceremony in Bristol. The night was going well until they announced I had won an award. Now, if I had jumped up in the time-honoured fashion I would have fainted on the spot. So I stood up very slowly and strolled to the stage to give my acceptance speech and then walked back to the table without falling over. So far, so good, but I was feeling poorly so Patsy and I left to go home. Patsy wanted me to call the doctor but I was due for a check-up at Southmead Hospital near my home in Bristol the next day.

While I am waiting for the doctor at Southmead, hospital staff bring me some food so I sit on the side of the bed and start eating. Suddenly, my face is in the plate of food. The patients think I always eat like that but the nurses realise I have fainted. Doctors and nurses instantly surround the bed and I hear them talking about moving me to the critical care unit. My kidneys are starting to fail rapidly and I can also hear them talking about my failing heart: unless I'm given a new one I'm going to die.

A nurse tells me that I'm being transferred to Papworth Hospital in Cambridge where I'll be cared for by Prince Charles's anaesthetist, and of course I go into Prince Charles impressions. In the end, to shut me up, they put a sheet over my head so I move into an Elephant Man routine – 'I am not an animal.' I'm dying and all I can think of is bad jokes.

I go back into the ward and they put a catheter up my willy so I can pee into a bag. As this is done by a very attractive female doctor, embarrassment is added to agony. I fight against having the catheter because for some mad reason of my own I think they should put it directly into my kidneys and that the medical staff have made some fundamental and totally inexplicable mistake.

Although they have told Patsy that I might not make the journey alive, mercifully they have not mentioned this to me. When she explains that they are trying to organise an air ambulance to take me to Papworth I ask, 'Why? What's wrong?' still totally unable to accept or understand that I am really very seriously ill. Unable to find a helicopter, they arrange an ambulance for myself and a car for Patsy. Alone in the back of the ambulance with a doctor and a nurse, the siren sounding, it finally starts to occur to me that this could be serious and I begin to look back over my life.

When we arrive, I'm rushed into intensive care and told that my family is all here. My beloved wife Patsy has arrived and my two daughters Samantha and Alison have brought my son Ryan down from Manchester. I am hooked up to machines, really out of it with drugs, and the reality turns into a dream. Six or seven doctors walk in and stand at the end of my bed, looking at the machine rather than me. There is an Indian chap, a Filipino, an African guy, a big tall blond guy in the middle. All nationalities appear to be represented in my own personal medical team and I start to think I am the new James Bond filming some bizarre torture sequence.

With a distinctly German accent, the man in the middle says, 'Velcome to Papworth.' All the expletives I have ever heard flash terrifyingly through my head and I think, What's happening? They tell me I am in good hands and that the reason I nearly died was because my kidneys were failing but they got me back and this is the start of the whole transplant saga.

My children come in expecting to find me at death's door, poor Ryan having been told by one health worker, 'You'd better hurry up, your dad's dying.' But the drugs have their effect and I am briefly at least revived. It's like a comedy routine where first one pops their head round the corner to have a look and then the others. The nurse says to my concerned offspring, 'Will you please tell your father to shut up. He has done nothing but talk since he came in here.'

But no one has spoken in those terms to me, and only the look on Patsy's face tells me to stop clowning around and do as I'm told. I learn some really good friends called Jean and John Mays have rushed over to our house to look after Patsy's elderly mother. I know it is really serious, otherwise they wouldn't have had to do that. At last I accept the seriousness of my situation. I still joke about it on the surface but underneath I am no longer laughing.

When the doctors leave, with me all hooked up to machines in the intensive care unit, the surgeon comes in. His name is Stephen Large and, although the coincidence is a bridge between us, his message is uncompromising. I am in trouble for not getting enough weight off, which has helped to cause this latest emergency. Unless I do as I'm told and the heart transplant is a success, I am a dead man. This is the real start of my fight to stay alive. I am just coming up to my 62nd birthday.

Still, when I was born I wasn't expected to live for 62 days.

CHAPTER ONE
The Carrot Thief

It's a long time ago, and it's not exactly one of the most hilarious gags I've come up with in a lifetime of trying to make people laugh, but I believe I can recall my very first joke. It was a sunny August day in 1946 on a bleak housing estate in Glasgow, and a five-year-old boy was trying hard not to show that he was frightened. I was lost and worried and a lady took pity on me. I admitted I didn't know where I was and she asked me my name. 'My name is McNamara, I'm the leader of the band,' I sang, mimicking the popular song of the day. I cannot remember whether or not my opening attempt at comedy received much of a response but, not for the last time, I was trying to see the funny side of a difficult situation.

My name was really Edward Hugh McGinnis, the son

of Jessie and Edward McGinnis, and I was born on 25 June 1941 in Rotten Row Hospital, Glasgow.

Jessie and Edward, better known as Teddy, were very proud of their first-born, although my father saw precious little of my early years as he was away in the Navy fighting Hitler. My father was a petty officer – or, as my mother preferred to colourfully to put it, a pissy officer – and when he came home on leave he used to regale me with exciting stories of fighting the Germans, Hun bullets flying everywhere and torpedoes missing his ship by inches. In later years, the war safely over, my father confessed quietly one day to me that his valiant service had been rather more like a five-year cruise and the action he had seen was certainly not on the high seas.

My father was given special leave when I was born and he was delighted when my mother produced a son weighing in at a healthy 8lb 7oz. But joy turned to concern when I contracted the often deadly disease diphtheria and was not expected to live. My weight plummeted to 5lb 12 oz and it looked for a time very much as if another young life was to be cut tragically short. Happily, for the first but by no means the last time in my life I cheated death and pulled through. Still, whenever people ask me about my weight, which does seem to hold a certain morbid fascination in some quarters, I always say my lightest ever was 5lb 12oz.

I soon recovered and grew into a cheerful toddler, lucky to be welcomed into a large and happy extended family. My mother had four sisters and three brothers, my father three brothers and a sister. I always had plenty of cousins to play with, and I'm still the only person I know to have two Uncle Bills.

My childhood memories are all happy ones. The earliest thing I can remember is sitting on my grandfather's foot and letting him bounce me up and down while I held on for dear life. In Scotland I think they call this Cokesey. I suppose I must have been one or two years old at the time.

My parents were both from Glasgow and the family story was that they met in a dance hall and quickly fell in love. I have a sister, Irene, who is six years younger than me and our little brother Brian came along much later. As he's 15 years younger than me I think he was 'once more for old time's sake'. I never told anyone at school at the time because in those days the very idea of your mum and dad doing anything like that was unthinkable. I was so embarrassed when my mum had a baby.

The family was very closely knit and nearly all my aunts and uncles were married with kids of their own. We all lived in a tenement: my dad always said that Glaswegians invented bunk beds out of necessity. We were like a huge tribe, a great, big happy family, and we should have had a revolving door on our house because people were always coming and going in such amazing numbers.

One of my mum's brothers went to Canada and joined

the army. I used to hear lots of stories about the success of Major Tom McKenna but I never met him. Uncle Charlie was a docker. One of my uncle Bills was called Trotsky because he was a bit of a communist, as were a lot of working people back then in Glasgow. He was a wanderer, and he was always disappearing and then turning up suddenly again out of the blue. Most of the women worked, too, apart from Minnie who used to look after me and take me to the pictures.

I was five years old when my dad came back from the war, which is when I discovered that my mother and all her family were Catholics, but my father was a Protestant. If we had lived in Birmingham or London this wouldn't have made any difference to my life, but in deeply sectarian Glasgow it changed everything. Because my dad was away at sea, my early years were spent with my mother's family at 55 Eglington Street and I was baptised into the Catholic Church and always going to mass. After my father's return I instantly became a Protestant and went to the local Protestant school. Even at that young age I was confused.

There was always a strong entertainment tradition in our family. Everyone could tell a tale or sing a song and two uncles, Hughie and John, were professional musicians. John played the violin in a band and we would gather round the radio on New Year's Eve and listen for 'Wee Johnnie McGinnis' being introduced for his solo. We were thrilled to hear his name broadcast.

After the war our home was 40 Wolsley Street,

Oatlands, on the third floor of a tenement building. It never occurred to me at the time but our living conditions were very cramped, with my parents sleeping in a recess off the kitchen while I occupied the back bedroom, where I was later joined by my sister Irene. The back of our flat overlooked the local Catholic school, St Bonaventure's, where my cousins all went. They would shout up from the playground to my mother, 'Auntie Jessie, are ye gonna throw us down a piece and jam' – a slice of bread and jam – which she would thoughtfully throw down to my hungry cousins.

But on religious days the atmosphere changed and suddenly it became all-important – occasionally even a matter of life and death – whether you were a Catholic or a Protestant. Then we would stop playing and start fighting, mimicking our elders who frequently took up weapons for their ancient cause. I saw young lads slashed with razors and others have their heads split open by bricks, all in the name of religion. I didn't understand what was going on back then and I understand it even less now. It certainly coloured my view of organised religion for life.

The next day we would all play happily together again as if nothing had happened. The deep-seated rivalries would be forgotten by us youngsters, until next year at least. I was brought up in a very religious community, and I was very religious myself for a time, but after witnessing such hatred and bigotry I do not have any time for religion and nor, I have to admit, do I believe in God.

Football was almost a religion to us street urchins, and while most of the kids in Glasgow supported Celtic or Rangers my dad persuaded me to join him and follow lowly Clyde, whose Shawfield Park ground was within walking distance of our tenement. 'Why Clyde?' I asked my father more than once. After all, it wasn't as if they were competing for the glamour associated with the two big sides. He claimed it was because they held the Scottish Cup longer than anyone else, having won it in 1939 and then keeping it until 1946, during which time the competition was suspended because of the war. So Clyde, or the Bully Wee as they are known, it was.

I suspect my father actually chose Clyde to avoid the religious bigotry that surrounds Celtic and Rangers. Glasgow was a very tough city and I think my father was concerned to see that I was being sucked into the street-gang life.

Once, a group of older boys put me through an initiation ceremony. I had to steal something from the local greengrocer's shop and in my first attempt at grand larceny I boldly snaffled a single carrot. My dad found out and gave me the biggest telling-off of my young life. But he still put the carrot into the stew. Neighbours would be coming up the stairs with coal that they'd nicked from the coal yard, but that was accepted because you couldn't afford to buy coal from the coalman. It was just that kind of life.

People came round all the time trying to sell knocked-off stuff. Yet, strangely, it was also a very religious life because we always went to the mission twice a week, although one of my main personal motivations for going was the cups of mushy peas they served. They were delicious.

Generally, it was all pretty strict, and of course the Catholic and Protestant divide was always very strong. One night a fella came down the road singing some sectarian song, I can't even remember which side it was about. The local tough guy came flying out of a snooker hall next to our tenement and started beating him up. It was daft. We kids didn't think anything about it. We didn't question the lunacy of families who were friends and neighbours suddenly becoming bitterly divided on religious grounds. It was simply a fact of life.

Even so, although Glaswegians have a very tough image, they are mainly very generous people. Years later, Syd and I used to meet them in the clubs and if they'd enjoyed the act they would come up and give you a fiver, however much you protested.

A lot of kids in Glasgow at the time were putting on little concerts in the courts behind the tenements. The *Daily Record* offered to publish the names of youngsters who raised any money for charity, so I joined forces with some friends for my first foray into showbusiness. There was plenty of raw talent with some fantastic singers, dancers and yodellers, and my mate Hughie did a brilliant impression of Al Jolson. As for me, I was hardly rated but I was content to play a clown in funny pyjamas and a painted face, especially when we raised 1/9d (less than 10p), sent it to the paper and duly had our names published. I was so proud to see 'Teddy McGinnis' in the paper. It was the thrill of a lifetime. How I wish I'd kept that cutting.

My memories are mostly of very good times. It might not be fashionable to admit it but I really enjoyed school, most of all because we spent every possible moment playing football. It was our passion and our season lasted for 52 weeks every year. We had vaguely heard of cricket but it was a weird English invention that held no interest for us. I did all the usual schoolboy things like throwing tar on to a fire and getting spits of red hot stuff back to scar my little legs for life. I also ran through a back court, in the dark, slap bang into an iron washing pole and needed 12 stitches in the resulting gash to my head.

In February 1952, my blissful Scottish life was shattered by astonishing news from my father – we were moving to England. I was dead against the move. I didn't know much about the English, but I knew I hated them. One of my uncles had confided more than once that the English were all 'puffs' and soft as shite.

My father had no interest in my racist protests. The decision had been taken and he explained that one of my mother's brothers, my other uncle Bill who lived in Manchester, had split up from his wife and was struggling to look after his two young sons Billy and Ian. My mother had agreed to go and help look after the boys, my father was going to get a job in Manchester and we would all make a new start south of the border.

I definitely didn't want to go to England, but you just accepted things in those days. You didn't have a counsellor to go and see. However, I think that my dad was perhaps much wiser than I ever gave him credit for at the time, and thought I was going down the wrong path. We were all street urchins and stealing was a part of life.

My father and mother also had their problems having married someone from another religion. It caused enormous difficulties and resentment. How dare you marry a Catholic? Or a Protestant? It was an outrage to some people and very unusual.

But Dad was a bit of a rebel. He didn't go to church much and didn't really believe in God, and I think I follow him in that. Even now when we go and visit where his ashes are scattered in a cemetery in Manchester, there's a rose bush with two of its branches giving a clear V sign, which pretty well sums up his attitude to a lot of the things in this world.

He was very much his own man. I remember going to a Labour Party meeting with him during which he launched into a colourful and fairly forcefully phrased question that came out as more of a condemnation of the main speaker. He wasn't afraid to speak his mind.

Dad never saw his own father, who was killed in the First World War near the Somme. After some research on the internet I located his grave and would love to have been able to take my father to the site but it was something we never got to do. My dad hated Winston Churchill and when everyone treated him as a hero Dad would insist he was nothing more than a ****ing warmonger. And he would go off on one.

CHAPTER TWO

The Accident

With all the trepidation of a family emigrating to the other side of the world, Irene, who was four, my mother and I boarded a Ribble bus in Glasgow that took us to Manchester. The journey seemed to go on forever and I remember we stopped in Preston which was my first landing on foreign soil. At first sight it seemed disappointingly similar to the landscape north of the border. My father was to follow on a week later after sorting out some final family business. Irene and I asked the usual questions posed by Scots venturing south of the border for the first time. Do they eat the same food as us? What language do they speak? Will the Queen be there?

Uncle Bill met us at the Chorlton Street bus station in Manchester and took us back to his house, 225

Maine Road. As the name suggests this was next door to the home of Manchester City Football Club, a noble institution which I was to come to know and love with a passion that sometimes surprises even those who think they know me best.

Bill's home was only a terraced house but it was a mansion to us because he had his own toilet. The prized water closet may have been in the back garden but only the people living in the house used it, whereas in Glasgow two other families had shared our loo.

It seemed a remarkable house. Although there were only two bedrooms, two families lived there quite comfortably. We even had a lodger. There was my uncle and my two cousins, Ian and Billy, me and my sister and mum and dad, and Frank McCoy the lodger. When Frank contracted TB, we all had to be screened and my mother was devastated when told she was negative as she thought it was bad news!

I was sent to Claremont Road School and there was an instant problem with my new classmates: they couldn't understand a word I said. I spoke with a very strong Glaswegian accent which can be impenetrable to Sassenachs, but I'm not sure they were trying too hard.

I can still recall the agony of my first day. A boy called Syd Johnson was assigned to look after me, my first piece of luck as he was a smashing lad who became a good friend. My language nightmare began when the teacher explained that to call the register we each had to shout out our number. I was 33, which still makes my flesh go cold because every time I called it out in my strong accent the whole class would collapse in gales of giggles. I don't think it was meant unkindly but I found it traumatic. I quickly went from being a brash confident boy to becoming sullen, moody and extremely shy.

There was a lot of mickey taking and that sparked quite a few fights. I soon discovered that the uncle who had told me all English were puffs and as soft as shite had made a serious mistake and I was beaten up in playtime. But I lost my accent in double-quick time and quickly became one of them.

By the time my father joined us I was in deep despair. I was crying myself to sleep every night and desperately wanted to go back to Glasgow. My dad told me to give it two weeks and if I still felt the same we would go home. He knew well enough that a fortnight is a very long time in the life of a ten-year-old and, with my ability to change accents and at least start to hold my own in the fighting stakes, I even started to enjoy myself.

What really clinched the success of the move was football. The good footballers had all been banned from playing owing to some trouble in the playground so in their absence, although I say it myself, I shone like a beacon. The first week my team won 2–0 and I scored both goals, the next week we won 4–0 and I scored all four. A star was born.

The following week the cricket season was about to start and, because of my football prowess, I was voted cricket captain. As I had never seen, much less played, a cricket match, this was to prove a problem, but for the moment I was a hero. Cricket just wasn't recognised in Glasgow. Mind you, I didn't tell anyone I had never played the game, and I was dead chuffed.

I took my 11-plus exams within a few days of arriving in Manchester. I nearly went to Manchester Grammar which would have been a real shock to my family as they most certainly couldn't have afforded the uniform. I was on the borderline in the exam. In those days there was a secondary modern school, then what they called a technical or central school, and then a grammar school. Most of the lads at Claremont Road went to the secondary modern just up the road but a couple of us 'brainy ones' went to Chorlton Central School. That was another trauma, and I cried every day. It was a whole bus ride from home.

One of my biggest culture shocks in Manchester concerned football. In Glasgow, you could stand outside a football ground, even Hampden Park when they were attracting crowds of 100,000, and say to any man in the queue, 'Will you lift me over, Mister?' They would cheerfully reach down and lift you over the turnstile and no one batted an eyelid. In Manchester, it was quite different. I asked someone to lift me over the turnstile and he looked at me as if I was from another planet, which in a way I was. They just didn't do that down there.

My father was a panel beater by trade and he got a

job in a garage in Hulme. It was supposed to be the place where Mr Rolls and Mr Royce first got together, although there didn't appear to be any trace of luxury left behind. Dad wasn't well paid but he enjoyed his work and eventually moved to Metro Vicks, a big engineering firm, for a couple of years before going back to work in garages. He always had a bad chest and had to stop work on health grounds when he was only 50. It seems so young now but when it happened I thought that my dad was mega-old. I was married by then and they were knocking down the houses where we lived and building new slums so my parents moved to Wythenshawe, where my father was astonished to discover he could get anything he wanted just by going in the pub at lunchtime. 'Have you got a phone? Could you get me a car?' He couldn't believe the dodges they all had in the pub.

Ted was a belligerent bugger. Viewing his relationship with my mother was like watching George Burns and Gracie Allen, or Alf Garnett and his wife, the so-called Silly Moo. It was a warm and fiery relationship and it was always very funny. My dad would be prattling on and my mum would effortlessly silence him with a brilliantly funny putdown. We got used to the arguments, they were never vicious.

At school, I never had the remotest ambition to become an entertainer or a comedian. My heroes were footballers, not comics. Mum worked in a cafe opposite the stage doors of the Hulme Hippodrome and the

Playhouse, a rep theatre, and I used to help her on Sundays. All the stars of the day came in so I met people like Al Read, Dave Morris, Bill Waddington and Joe Gladwin, and I suppose it must have given me my first taste of showbusiness. They were all great characters who seemed to be enjoying an exciting life so I suppose unconsciously it did get me interested, but I never gave it much thought at the time. They would sometimes hand out a ticket to the shows and I would often go on my own to see a variety act.

I was definitely not impressed by The Beverley Sisters. There was only one power socket in the cafe and I was sitting listening to an England match on the radio. It was bleeding freezing in there and The Beverley Sisters came in and one of them said, 'Can we have the fire on, please?' It was a bit of a cheek, considering one of them was married to England skipper Billy Wright. But the radio was unplugged and I had to stop listening to the match.

I loved the radio, particularly *The Goons*, but I was not interested in showbusiness. If you'd asked me what I liked I would have said football. One of our teachers, Mrs Roberts, used to ask me to be in the school play but I thought all that acting nonsense was for wimps. The school play? Do me a favour, what sort of a lad do you think I am? Then she came back one day and said, 'Ah, McGinnis, we're one short, we've been let down. Would you join our play?' She was so appealing I found I couldn't say no.

'Well, all right, Miss, I'll do it.'

My mates were laughing. 'Aw, Macca, you're not going in the school play, are you?'

'Well, only because she's desperate.'

I pretended to be reluctant but actually I loved every minute of it. I have a photo somewhere of me with Kevin Comrie, who went on to become a headmaster, and the girl who was the real talent of our school, Sylvia Farmer. She played the cornet in the Beswick Prize Band when she was only 14 and she would play at Maine Road one week and at Old Trafford the next week. We all cheered when Sylvia was on a television talent show and mentioned our school. She was like a star and everyone fancied her.

After that, I was in every school play. A critic came one year and he was going to judge us on the performance. He said something flattering about someone that was quite nice and then he started to mention me – I was playing a jester. Being super-sensitive, I was worried what he was going to say about me. But he praised the lad in the list before me who played the king and then said he was sorry, but he had made a mistake, and he had been talking about me, Edward McGinnis. The trouble was, I hadn't been listening properly so I couldn't remember his verdict in detail.

It was a mixed school and they taught you proper ballroom dancing with real live girls. There was no alternative as rock'n'roll was yet to arrive. You had to dance with your classmates, which was so embarrassing and scary at that age. Even worse, at the start you had to step forward and ask a girl to dance. If you were slow, like me, all the pretty ones were long gone by the time you plucked up the courage.

I dreaded the experience, but I'll never forget the relief when I asked a girl called Joan Davenport to dance with me and she accepted. I was so grateful to her for saying yes that, rather than chance my arm with any other girls, I asked Joan every time for the next two years.

People always imagine I'm brimming with confidence, but as a teenager I was very shy. There was no thought of taking the girls out. We had no money for that and in any case we were not advanced like the kids of today.

I don't recall taking many girls out when I was at school. I was always with a gang of my mates and we were always much more interested in football. I suppose I was always lusting after girls from a distance but I just didn't have the nerve to ask them, as I was extremely shy as a teenager. My passion was football: I just loved the game and I think I still do.

Two people had a big influence on my early life. One was a teacher called Mr Musker, at Chorlton Central School, who inspired me even though he was a tough disciplinarian. He taught maths as well as taking us for sports and was a tough, fair bloke. I thought I was one of his favourites, but one day, just after I had learned to whistle, I was showing off my new skill with a blast that shattered the calm classroom, and I got the strap. I thought, You can't give me the strap. I'm captain of the football team. But Mr Musker didn't have any favourites and we respected him for that.

They weren't all quite so inspirational, though. One teacher, Mr Bunnidge, said to me in my final year, 'As for you, McGinnis, all you will end up doing is selling programmes outside Wembley for the Cup Final.'

'Well, I don't mind that, sir,' I replied, 'just working one day a year.'

While Syd Johnson helped me at Clairmont Road Junior School, Geoff Bray was invaluable after my move to Chorlton Central. I was upset by all the change and crying, so my dad found this lad who was already at the school. Geoff, although a year older, took to me and really paved my way, and we became firm friends.

We used to get off the bus in Maine Road and walk home past Wilbraham Road Junior School and often saw a particular young kid playing football. He was so outstanding you couldn't help but notice him, and we used to stop and watch. He turned out to be Neil Young, who went on to play for Manchester City and scored the winning goal in the 1969 FA Cup Final. Geoff and I obviously had an eye for talent.

When I was 14, I went to play football for this under-18s team called Brighton Lads Club, which was a big difference from the school team. It toughened me up and brought me on in leaps and bounds. Four years is a massive difference at that age. We had moved to Overton Street in Hulme and I had no mates around there because it was so far from the Maine Road area. I was just left on my own all the time, so it was very lonely. A lad in our street asked me if I wanted to play for Brighton Lads. I enjoyed that, but the team disbanded after a year and I had nowhere to play and I asked my friend Derek Valentine if I could go with him to play for Norbrook Boys Club in Wythenshawe. It was an under-16s team and by then I was 15. I was playing with lads of my own age and, as I had really improved, I did well with Norbrook. I used to go up three or four times a week, on the 108 bus, which coincidentally stopped just outside what I later learned was the home of a young chap called Cyril Mead. But I didn't meet him then.

Then came that embarrassing realisation when my brother was born, when I was 15. I thought all that sort of stuff had finished years ago. And when Brian was born at home I felt desperately uncomfortable at school. It's hard to credit how silly and prudish I must have been at the time.

The other great influences on my early life was Frank Shatwell, or Mr Shatwell, as I respectfully called him, who ran Norbrook Boys Club as if it were Manchester City. Our team were all around 17 and just starting to go into the local pubs. He brought us all into the office and asked us if we had been drinking. A few of us shamefacedly admitted that we had and he said gravely, 'Footballers should not be drinking.' He really kept us on the straight and narrow. I have a lot to thank him for.

It was Mr Shatwell who suggested I try some of the new 'continental' boots, as they were called. I couldn't afford them, of course, so Frank lent me £3 which I was going to pay him back at a shilling a week. I paid him dutifully for a few weeks but then I was really hard up and asked if I could pay him the following week. I never did, and I have had a tremendous guilt complex about that ever since. The Puma boots I bought, however, were wonderful, like slippers after the great heavy pair I'd been using for years.

Some lads did get into trouble. Four from our team were put in borstal for burglary and I never had a clue it was going on. I think it was maybe because I was going back to Moss Side at nights and didn't see them much outside football, but it really shook me up: that could have been me if it hadn't been for the Mr Shatwells of this world. I've been lucky because there are so many wrong roads I could have gone down.

When I was 15, Mr Musker sent me for a trial with Manchester School Boys. I thought I did OK, but on the bus one of the kids told me, 'They've picked a 14-year-old lad instead of you, Macca.'

I was a bit miffed because I was 15 and reckoned I was better than anyone younger than me. They pointed to his name on the list, Norbert Styles, a weedy-looking kid with glasses who didn't look like a footballer to me.

His dad had a funeral director's business and, searching frantically for reasons to explain why Styles had been preferred to me, I decided that must have swung it. They've got money, I thought. Years later, watching Nobby running around Wembley with the World Cup, I didn't feel quite so sad. Maybe he was just that little bit better than me.

I stayed on another year at school after I reached the leaving age of 15 because I was happy there and I didn't have a clue what I wanted to do afterwards. I needed to get seven subjects in my school certificate to stay on, which I somehow managed. I even became a school prefect.

Eventually I left in July 1957, aged 16, but I still didn't know what I wanted to do. My parents kept telling me to get a trade and I succumbed to that after a while, applying to become an apprentice at Metro Vicks. It went on to become AEI, coincidentally where Frank Shatwell worked. I think the site where it used to stand is now where the Trafford Centre attracts thousands of shoppers every day, but in 1957 it was a massive engineering firm.

My first job had been working for a clothing firm called Sparrow Hardwicks in Manchester, on the pretext that I was going to become a buyer when I was about 50. However, it was just a fill-in time dodge until I started at Metro Vicks in November. I worked on the reception desk at Sparrow Hardwicks and then had a go as the lift operator before being moved into the despatch department right down in the bowels of the place. I hated it everywhere I worked. Mercifully, it was just from July to November.

When I finally started at Metro Vicks, it was just like an extension of school because you spent a year in the training department learning all the skills. You had a month being a welder, a month doing tool-making, a month doing electric stuff, and so on. Even then I didn't know what I wanted to be and worked in various different departments. At 21, you had to decide which department you wanted to work in, then go and ask its foreman if you could join. I started on £1 11/6. It wasn't much, because once Syd and I got started on the clubs we were getting a fiver a night, almost as much as for a 40-hour week.

But work did give me a footballing chance. Harry Goodwin, Manchester City's chief scout at the time, worked at Metro Vicks and sent me for a trial with City. It was a shilling there and back on the train to Piccadilly and I didn't have enough money for the return fare, so I had to walk the three miles back home from the city centre.

All the kids who were signed on lined up to get their travelling expenses. Geoff Fry, a footballing pal from Norbrook who was on City's books, lined up, so I did as well. When the guy paying the money out came to me, he said, 'Your name isn't down here, are you sure you're signed on?'

I admitted I wasn't and didn't get the money for the fare home.

Next time I couldn't even afford to get there and Harry came looking for me at work. 'Why haven't you been for the trial?' he asked. 'They wanted you to.'

I said I couldn't afford it and he suggested my dad would help me but at the time we didn't have the money at all. Had it been Maine Road I could have walked there but it was out in Urmston, which is miles away.

Happily, my football career continued to prosper and, thanks to Mr Shatwell, I won a place in the Manchester Boys Clubs side. It was an honour and I was very proud. In fact, Norbrook was proud because we were one of the smaller clubs and that year had three players in the Manchester side – yours truly, Geoff Fry and Charlie Chadwick. Part of the deal was that, if you were injured or hurt playing football, you could go to Old Trafford and the physio would look after you. Cynics might claim this apparent benevolence was so that Manchester United could have their pick of the best young players, but I couldn't possibly comment.

After I injured the cartilage in my left knee I was duly sent off to Old Trafford to receive treatment from Bert Whalley, the physio at the time. He brought me in and of course there were real footballers all over the place. I didn't see Bobby Charlton or Duncan Edwards – I think they were away in the army at the time – but all of the others, people such as David Pegg and Eddie Coleman, most of them household names, were around. I couldn't believe how young they all were. They just looked like the older lads I played football with, yet if you saw them on the pitch they seemed like giants.

Two weeks later the terrible Munich Disaster happened and many of these fine men, including poor old Bert Whalley, were dead. It was a terrible shock. Manchester United wasn't my team but I was absolutely devastated by the news. The whole city was. There were no sick jokes like there would be today. There was just overwhelming grief. Everybody was affected by it.

I must have been a very slow developer because I was 17 before I asked a girl out. My career as a great romancer was rudely interrupted, however, when I had a traumatic accident. It happened in such bizarre circumstances, as if it was almost meant to be.

I was out in Wythenshawe with the lads, Charlie Williams, Derek Valentine and the rest of my mates. We had stayed at Charlie's house because we had played football, then I always cycled home on Sunday night. This night, I discovered I had a puncture. I needed a bike to go to work the next day as I didn't have any money for a bus fare, so Derek lent me his.

Next day I was cycling along to work in the rush hour on a strange bike. Set in the road were big railway lines to carry the heavy stuff that used to travel between factories, criss-crossing the old tram lines. There were also big holes left in the road that were occasionally filled in with pitch or tar, but over the years these had worn out.

As I was riding along, my front wheel became trapped in one of these nasty little ruts and I fell off. A bus was right behind me as I crashed to the ground and, although the bus driver swerved out to try to miss me, he clipped my ankle. It was a nightmare. There was blood everywhere, but at first I was more embarrassed than anything else because my jeans had been ripped off and I was trying to cover myself to keep decent. I can remember my neighbour Les, with his motorbike and sidecar, actually coming alongside me as I was lying on the road shocked and hurt. I didn't quite realise what had happened to me and Les was panicking because he didn't want to be late for work. It was terrible, but at least I got my name in the paper.

I was rushed to Manchester Royal Infirmary in an ambulance. I was amazingly lucky and had only cracked a bone in my ankle. They strapped it all up and dressed it and put it in a plaster but I was still in pain. They said, 'Don't worry, we will take the plaster off in a few days.'

When they took the plaster off, all the skin on my right-hand side was horribly infected. They had to cut all the skin away to get rid of the infection and graft skin back on from my shoulder. It wasn't the best skin graft in the world by a long chalk, and it caused me some psychological problems that today would surely be taken quite seriously, but weren't thought much of at the time.

My mother brought a letter into the hospital to say

that I had been selected to play for England Boys Clubs. Now there's me, Scottish, wondering what on earth to do – what would my dad say? – though I obviously couldn't play with my injury anyway.

One of the doctors knew Matt Busby, who sent in a book with the autographs of the entire Manchester United team. It was a kind and generous gesture but I'm ashamed to admit that it didn't impress me one bit because I was a confirmed Manchester City fan. I wish I had kept it, of course, because now it would be a collectors' item.

All sorts of strange things happened around that time. Earlier that day my sister and I had a big argument, as brothers and sisters do. In a rage she had shouted at me, 'I hope you get run over today,' a remark she's never forgotten and I'm afraid it has haunted her ever since, although we both know full well that it was only said in a moment of childish anger and meant nothing.

Desperate to find employment, my father had gone down to Oxford to work for Morris Cowley and was away. Mum had young Brian to look after so it was difficult for her. I was in hospital for nine weeks, largely because of this horrendous skin graft. That was when the weight started to pile on and the whole course of my life began to change. When I came out of hospital, my mates and I started to go out to pubs drinking a lot.

My leg wept fluid for ages after the accident and I had to keep going back to Manchester Royal to get it dressed. After months of that, one of the doctors looked into it. 'How long has this been going on?' he wanted to know. I explained I kept putting dressings on but it kept just seeping through. He treated me with a powder that dried it up, but medical treatment wasn't so great back in those days.

I had been for a football trial at Bury just before the accident. A scout watched us play for Norbrook and invited Charlie Chadwick, one of the lads on the team, to go for a trial at Bury but didn't say anything to me at the time. As I was cycling home through a park, the scout stopped me and asked me to come along with Charlie.

Charlie was a good player but had very poor eyesight and wore his glasses to play. He was a centre forward and scored lots of goals but that night the coach told him to take off his glasses. I was the opposing centre half, marking Charlie in the trial, and, as he couldn't see well enough to control the ball, I had a pretty easy time. He was literally in the dark and I was left looking like Franz Beckenbauer, doing well enough to be offered £8 a week to sign as a semi-pro. But the week after that I had my accident and the opportunity went out of the window.

The accident was a major blow, and I lost my confidence. I attempted to play football but had lost my fitness and put on weight – I used to cycle everywhere and was very, very fit, which until then had kept my weight down – and was never anywhere near as good a player as I had been before. I lost heart, and the team disintegrated when we all reached 18. Afterwards, I spent more time drinking my pints of beer and going to dance halls, and the weight just piled on.

Looking back, of course, I bitterly regret the accident that ended my footballing dreams. But would I have made it as a soccer player? We'll never know. Some friends say kind things about my abilities on the pitch and I have happy memories. But it's a familiar story. The older you get, the better you were!

CHAPTER THREE

When Eddie Met Cyril

I first met Syd Little when I was 18 years old. My accident had ended any hopes of playing football for Manchester City and Scotland, and a great deal of my energy went into nights out with the lads, though we were no competition for the binge-drinking youngsters of today. In those days, you had to be able to hold your beer and my fast-expanding frame bore witness to my capacity for holding rather more than my share.

Most of my gang at the time are still friends to this day. Gradually, we somehow merged with another gang that included a young chap called Cyril Mead. Syd, as he was known, swaggered around in such a geeky, oddball way that at first I thought he must be incredibly hard, with enormous confidence to stand up and sing to his own guitar accompaniment in some of the roughest pubs in Manchester. Anyone who dared to look that weird must be really tough. How wrong can you be?

His act was highly individual. The first time I saw him singing at Brooklands Trade and Labour Club, where his dad was on the committee, I thought he was hopeless. He sang 'Big Bad John', but not as anyone remembers it. He turned it into a skiffle song which I thought was completely the wrong way to sing it. Then he sang 'Muleskinner Blues', one of my favourite songs, and my ears really pricked up. I thought, How does he know 'Muleskinner Blues'? It was quite an obscure country and western song. That made me interested in Syd and I suppose it was the first link between us. Even though he did sing it too fast.

Even as lads, long before I ever dreamed of a career as a comedian, Syd always seemed to be the butt of all the jokes. He was just that sort of guy. And I always seemed to get the blame for most of the pranks, but I wasn't always guilty. Honest!

One of the worst was on a holiday trip to the Isle of Man when someone peed in Syd's beer. We all had bottles of beer on the table; evidently they didn't have pint glasses in that part of the island for some reason. One of Syd's mates, a joker called Alfie, thought it would be hilarious to pee in Syd's bottle, even pouring a little bit of frothy beer on top to cover it up. Syd drank the lot, which perhaps says as much about the quality of the beer as it does about his sense of taste. We let him in on the joke afterwards and ever since he has blamed me. After all, I could have stopped Alfie, couldn't I?

As teenagers, we were always getting in fights, even Syd. He started a fight once, trying to pull a girl. Next minute, her boyfriend turned up, saying what are you doing trying to get off with my girlfriend. Suddenly we're all out in the street and a big fight is going on. With his highly developed sense of personal safety Syd somehow managed to walk away unscathed.

It's hard to pin down how our partnership began. Syd was always trying to sing in the pubs and I was always keen to interrupt and take the mickey, and sing a song myself... if I had enough Dutch courage. I think the first time was at a pub in Timperley. I had about five pints inside me and it seemed like a bright idea to ask Syd to back me in a rendition of 'Livin' Doll'. Sorry, Cliff.

It wasn't long before my gang and Syd's teamed up and became regulars at the Stonemason's Arms, until we got barred. Somehow, late at night, we found ourselves standing up there together and people were laughing so I kept clowning around. We entertained together at Brooklands Trade and Labour Club where we were memorably billed as Cyril Mead And Friend. No one even knew my name. Gradually, an uneasy partnership formed between us. We were friends but we were not really close at first.

The evening I remember most clearly from those heady days of youth was at Timperley Labour Club. Syd was having problems with his amp so he asked the group he was sharing the bill with if he could borrow one of their amplifiers. Charitably, they refused so Syd was panicking. His elder brother Peter, a bit of an electrician, was trying to repair Syd's amp.

That night, Peter came up to me and asked, 'Will you get up with our Syd?'

We'd done odd little bits together, nothing major, but I'd had a few pints which was enough to give me some courage. So I said, 'Yeah, I don't mind.'

I got up and, after only a few seconds, Syd's amp broke down once and for all, so I started taking the mickey out of Syd, and the Timperley Labour Club liked it. The audience roared with laughter so I clowned around some more. There's nothing like the sound of genuine laughter that you have created out of nothing. It's a wonderful sound and I liked it straight away.

Afterwards, the club secretary came up to us and said, 'I want to book you back, you went down so well.' I thought he just meant Syd, and Syd started to look at his diary but the secretary said, 'No, I want both of you together.' I was convinced it was a one-off but then he said, 'I'll give you six pounds.' I was stunned. It was definitely an offer I couldn't refuse. 'What are you called?' asked the club secretary. We were put down as Syd and Eddie and that was our early name.

I loved the applause and enjoyed the bonus of extra money, but it was quite a while before either of us considered it seriously as a career. We found ourselves in growing demand around Manchester and our pub earnings soon became much larger than either my pay from Metro Vicks or Syd's wages as a painter and decorator. Very soon we were gaining a reputation of sorts around Manchester. We started entering talent contests and at the Royal Naval Club, Wythenshawe, we came second. The actress Pat Phoenix presented the prizes. When we met her again, almost 20 years later, she remembered the evening very well. What a lovely lady.

We were plunged into an exotic world for which nothing could have prepared us. I was still very shy but I found I could hide my shyness behind my entertainment identity. Up there as the life and soul of the pub, ruthlessly ridiculing Syd for laughs, I found I could relax and enjoy myself. I loved the applause and the warmth that can come from an audience on a good night.

Of course, there were plenty of indifferent nights as well, but we knew we had something. We just weren't at all sure what on earth it was, of course. We hadn't prepared our stage performances with precision and rehearsal. We simply settled for a light-hearted extension of ourselves that for some peculiar reason seemed to make people laugh. We loved it. Full of energy and the confidence of youth, we borrowed pop songs, jokes, take-offs and dance routines from wherever we could find them. Experienced comics would often take us to one side and give us a gag, or show us a way of improving part of our act. We weren't proud and we were being paid.

The Syd and Eddie Show appeared at Trafford Park Working Men's Club where our supporting comic was a very sharp lad from Liverpool called Jimmy Tarbuck. He asked us if we would open the show as we did music and if we would mind closing the show as he had to get up early. It took us ages to work out that we had been conned and we have had many a laugh with Jimmy about it since.

Bernard Manning's Embassy Club was one of our early bookings, an educational experience whichever way you looked at it. I remember going, determined to demand we were paid £100 a week, but bottling out and asking for £60. We got £55 and Bernard really made you work for it – but who cared? Syd and I did somersaults of joy because £55 was a fortune to us in those days.

Bernard also made us work in his two other clubs, the Palladium and the Wilton, as well as in the Embassy, and still said he was overpaying us.

We are good friends to this day. Bernard might cross the barriers of good taste more than just occasionally but his heart's in the right place. He just can't resist a cruel gag. I remember after Rolling Stone Brian Jones drowned in a swimming pool, Bernard cracked ruthlessly that it was the first bath he'd had in years.

In the early days in Manchester, there were some amazing characters. Muscleman Tony Brutus, who was billed as The Strongest Man In Britain was persuaded to be hung on stage by a club owner. Brutus's wife came home early one day to find him strung up by a noose from the banisters and ran down the road screaming in hysterics. Tony followed frantically yelling, 'I'm only rehearsing.'

When the night of the hanging arrived, they had built a scaffold in the Liverpool club where he was appearing and Tony was all dressed up as a robber with a hooped pullover and mask. The place was heaving as the club owner dramatically read out Tony's so-called crimes. Just before it came to the big moment when he was going to pull the lever, two policemen arrived and shouted, 'There will be no hanging in here tonight.' The owner could see all his profits disappearing at the last minute so he pulled the lever anyway. Tony had been distracted by all the commotion and wasn't ready when the rope tightened round his neck, so he almost did get hanged!

Tony was only 5ft 3in tall but he really was strong. He was set upon by four thugs one night just as he was packing his gear into the car and all of them finished up in hospital.

The comedians were the ones I loved, perhaps because they all seemed to be slightly on the edge of the law. So many of my memories of those days are of laughter. One character, whose name I can't for the life of me recall, had built up a lot of work on the cruise ships and he was convinced he was on the verge of making it big in America. He gave us his card after one meeting and it said, ALL COMMUNICATIONS, 113 HOLLYWOOD BOULEVARD, LOS ANGELES, UNITED STATES OF AMERICA, OR 12 INKERMAN STREET, ROTHERHAM. I remember showing this card to Frank Carson and then standing back in the gales of laughter.

Then there was a guy called Eddie Grant who would always try to corner the sympathy vote. I first saw him one night at the Yew Tree Hotel. He broke down halfway through his act and started crying and said that his mother had just died. He was so upset someone passed a pint pot around and we all bunged money into it. Then, a couple of weeks later, he was distraught because his father had tragically died. This happened wherever he went but gradually people would crack.

The Yew Tree was run by a real hard nut called Frank Tansey. Some time later, Eddie broke down with another desperate story of woe and agony, the only difference was that this time it was genuine, and his mother had actually died. Tansey got on to him mercilessly, 'Look, Eddie, she died last month, you can't pull that stunt again.'

When we were semi-pro we would just go on in the clothes we arrived in. As we gradually became more professional, we thought we had better look the part, so we bought cardigans! We would take them off, put our jackets on and go to the next club where we would get changed among the crates at the back. Acts coming from playing the halls would be astonished. They would ask, 'Where's the dressing room?' and we'd say 'You're in it.' We didn't use make-up for a long time.

We weren't exactly successful but we turned professional on the basis that we had three months' work ahead of us, with at least £20 a week each coming in. It was good money if you were living with your mother and not doing anything, but when you were on the road and you had to stay in digs and you were going out all the time it wasn't much, even back then. Everyone was like that. We knew lots of comics and groups and different acts and they were all in the same boat. They could earn the cash but they were spending just as fast as it came in. And when you're in 'showbusiness' it seems only natural to 'show off'.

Although we had loads of trials and tribulations, I know I couldn't have laughed as much in any other job. There have been stresses and arguments along the way but we have laughed like drains together so many times.

A double act is a weird thing and there have been highs and lows, but many times I have thought it is great to have a partner. In the early days, we were like Siamese twins. In fact, back then lots of people thought we were gay, although we were totally oblivious to it, because we never had any girlfriends for quite a long time and we were always together! Showbusiness does attract some fairly flamboyant individuals, even though Syd and I were hardly ever that.

One comic clearly got the wrong idea. We admired this guy's act and afterwards he asked us if we wanted to go back to his flat for a cup of tea. We were delighted: we had only been in the business for two minutes and he was asking us back to his flat in Whalley Range. We got there to find a young lad in bed and it was clear that the intention was for us all to end up in there with him. The penny dropped and I said to Syd it was time to exit stage left, fast. Which we did.

We were lucky to have each other. Over the years, lots of people told me I should ditch Syd and go solo but I don't think we would have had the success we did if I'd done that. We needed each other in some of those tough areas.

Work came in from all directions in those days. I remember going to Bolton, to the club where Peter Kay filmed *Phoenix Nights*, the Old Veteran Club in Farmouth. I had been on a works trip and on the way back stopped for a drink in the Old Vets Club. After a few drinks, I asked if I could get up on stage. I thought I would just sing a couple of songs and I started skylarking around.

With no pressure, it went down well and the concert secretary said he would like to book me. I had to explain I was in a double act called Syd and Eddie. I wasn't sure how much to ask for and he offered seven guineas. Wow! That was a breakthrough. We had never been paid more than a fiver before between the two of us. But perhaps it wasn't the greatest coup of our professional lives because it cost us seven quid in a taxi to get there and back.

After the accident, I couldn't play football so I had a lot more time on my hands. I used to go to the Locarno in Sale with my mates and plucked up enough courage to ask a girl out. We went to the pictures a few times but nothing physical ever happened.

It's hard to convey how shy and backward I was when it came to the opposite sex. But times have changed tremendously in my life in that respect. In those days, you definitely didn't assume that you were going to end up in bed with a girl just because you were going out together. For a start there wasn't anywhere to go. Our house was always pretty overcrowded and people tended not to go out very often. Those younger days were incredibly innocent. I was never the best puller of girls in our gang. I was pretty shy and I was tiny as well, especially when the girls were wearing high heels.

Then I met a girl called Pat Blake. She was in our group and somehow, without any hint of a romantic overture from me, we started going out together. We had some laughs and I thought we made a good couple, and in a very short space of time we got engaged. Looking back, if I'm honest, I think she was more of a friend than a girlfriend. She was a nice girl and I liked her, but my main motivation was fear.

For some strange reason I was desperately worried about being left on the shelf. My mate Jimmy Brown had a sister called Margery, and Pat was her friend, which was how I first got to know her. We were at Margery's house and the record player was broken so I repaired it for them. Pat was quite impressed with my electrical skills, which was certainly a shock for me.

Everyone seemed to be in couples and getting married and I just didn't want to be left behind. In those days if you got past 21 and you didn't have a girlfriend people started to think that there was something weird about you. Looking back I never ever really thought about what I was doing. Getting engaged and then getting married was just what you did. It was a natural progression.

By then, me and Syd were working more and more, so Pat and I were putting money into our account at the building society, because that was what you did to get yourself a house. We didn't have a car, as that was beyond our reach at that time, although I did start taking driving lessons.

Pat and I got engaged and, in the summer of 1963, as all of the single lads in our gang prepared to go off on a hard-drinking holiday to the Isle of Man, I found I couldn't go with them because I was with Pat. In my heart I wanted to be with the lads, but I thought this engaged business was a vital part of growing up and something you simply had to do. First, you got a fiancee and then you had to spend time with her in preparation for a home and a family and the prospect of gradually turning into your parents. I wish I could say I questioned these perceived wisdoms of working-class life but the truth is I just went along with it like everyone else.

As my mates headed off with another round of heavy drinking and late-night frolics at the top of the agenda, I set off towards Rhuddlan in North Wales with Pat and her family to holiday in a converted railway carriage. Syd and I laughed a lot at the idea of spending a holiday in a stationary railway carriage but it was no joke when the time arrived. That trip was to change my life.

I went along with the idea of a family holiday but I was used to going away with the lads for a holiday, so this was different. To put it politely, it was very boring. Pat's family evidently enjoyed listening to the radio and reading books and not going out. They didn't even want to go to the local pub. This was not the sort of holiday I could relate to so I quickly became a bit fed up with the whole experience, in spite of a visit to Llandudno to see The Beatles on a variety bill. There was no screaming and the Fab Four were first on at 6.10pm. It was great, but it was very much an isolated highlight.

I wanted to go out and I suggested we went off into Rhyl for the day; hardly Las Vegas but at least there was a bit of life there. Pat didn't want to do anything like that so I went off on my own one night. Funnily enough, I met a girl who I did eventually end up going out with in this pub in Rhyl. I really enjoyed my bit of freedom, but back in the railway carriage you could cut the atmosphere with a knife.

I am a very loyal person. I knew it was not going to work but I was worried that, if we split up, I wouldn't have a girlfriend and I'd have to start again. There was a lot of peer pressure when your mates all seemed to be courting or even getting married. I'd go to weddings and think, Crikey, I'm 22 and I'm on my own. Life was different then.

But it just was not happening between me and Pat. It didn't help that her parents didn't understand me at all. 'Why isn't he working in a factory like normal people?' they wanted to know all the time.

We were due to go home on the Saturday, and on the Friday I finally faced up to the fact that our relationship and the railway carriage had one important thing in common – neither of them was going anywhere. I went home the next day and I met my mates, who thought it was hilarious.

'Where have you been?'

'I've been in a railway carriage in Wales.'

Roars of laughter and derision. That was it.

Pat and I had money we had saved in the building society. It was mainly cash that I had put in, but being a congenital soft touch as usual I gave her half of it, but now at last I had a few hundred quid to get a motor of my own.

I went with my dad to Colmore Motors in Manchester and found a Minivan with 4,000 miles on the clock. It was love at first sight between me and 9223ND, and that was it: that was Syd and Eddie on the road. We drove thousands of miles in that van. All of a sudden we could go to Yorkshire, Blackpool, the north-east, anywhere we wanted. I can still remember feeling the fantastic freedom that little Minivan gave us. It changed our lives overnight. And it gave us some memorable moments.

We had one wild night out in February 1964. We had turned pro the previous October. I still hadn't passed my driving test but we didn't bother with L plates or anything like that. We did a gig at the Lancashire Cricket Club and there was a man I used to work with in the audience. We had a good night and my friend from work asked us back to his house for a drink. He woke his wife up so she could have the pleasure of making us some sandwiches. We had a good session and then we headed off back to Syd's house. Foolishly, I said to Syd, 'Do you fancy a drive?' I think he'd started taking lessons at the time and, to be fair, he drove quite well.

We went all round Manchester Airport, all round the country lanes as they were then, and, as we were getting close to Syd's house, he wanted to turn right and wasn't sure whether that meant the indicator switch went up or down. While solving this mind-numbing problem, there was a bit of a wobble in the van's direction and next thing we were pulled up by a policeman on a motorcycle. I had an inspiration. I rushed round to the driver's side and told Syd to get over, and then tried to pretend I had been driving.

The policeman was not impressed. 'Do you think I am ***ing blind?' he asked bluntly. He turned to Syd and asked, 'Have you been drinking?'

Syd admitted he'd had a few, something of an understatement.

'Well, walk down that white line and show me if you are fit to drive.'

Syd very carefully strode down the white line. The policeman turned to me and asked if I had my licence. As I hadn't, he ordered me to produce it at my local police station. But he hadn't told Syd to stop walking and by now he was nearly home.

The copper looked up and saw Syd was about half a mile down the road. 'Oi,' he shouted. Syd came back and the copper was not surprised to discover he didn't even have a licence. We were in trouble and he ordered us both to report to our local police station. Then he let us drive off home!

We weren't legless but we were both well over the limit. Well, that's it, I thought, our careers are over. We've only been in the business about five minutes but we won't be able to work if we can't drive.

The next day we went to the local station, and the copper on duty was a mate of ours who we'd done police charity work for. He was sympathetic and, fortunately, the copper who had stopped us was a pal of his. He rang him up and mentioned us running the charity show, and everything was quietly dropped. Those were the days.

But my memory is still of Syd walking carefully down that white line as if his life depended on it. Goodness knows how far he would have gone if the policeman hadn't shouted him back.

In March 1964, we had our big chance to join the pop explosion that was rocking the country. We were appearing at Offerton Palace Club near Stockport when a man from Decca Records approached us. Decca had recently rejected The Beatles so anyone who sang and got a round of applause in a northern club was signed up. We were teamed up with top producer Mike Leander to record my beloved 'Muleskinner Blues' in a proper London studio. We were so excited. We had never been to London before, let alone into a proper studio.

Syd brought along his guitar and amplifier but as soon as we arrived Mike Leander introduced us to the guitarist on the session, a young guy named Jimmy Page. This was well before the days of Led Zeppelin, but even I could tell he had the edge over Syd musically. We had all the top session men involved and the Ladybirds were our backing singers. We recorded four songs altogether and they sounded fantastic. Anyone who has ever been in a recording studio, however, will tell you that when the music is played back on the giant speakers it always sounds great.

We were dead chuffed and off we went back to Manchester to wait for a call to record our spot for *Top Of The Pops*. We told everybody about our record but a few weeks later we got a call from Decca to redo the vocals. This was no problem, just another trip down to London. When we arrived in the studio, Mike Leander turned all the music off to let us listen to our voices. We sussed the problem straight away – we couldn't sing. I was very embarrassed and swore I would never sing again. Needless to say, the record was never released and people were asking us for years when it was coming out.

Life was never boring. We were excited by the prospect of two weeks in Paris entertaining the troops at nearby American bases. We were like two little boys lost when we arrived in Paris. We had two days off as soon as we got there so we just wandered round with our eyes out on stalks.

Communication with the locals was difficult. I remarked to Syd that one of the major problems with the French was that they did not speak English. The only thing we understood on a menu was 'une salade' and when it came it was only a piece of lettuce. We couldn't even find a way to explain that we wanted coffee with milk. Food was available at the army bases but we wanted to eat in Paris when we got back from work. An American eventually taught us to say '*deux jambon omelettes et deux cafe au lait*' but when we parroted it out at a confused-looking waiter he responded, 'Oh, do you want milk in your coffee?' He was from Manchester.

We just about got away with our act for the American troops by sticking to country and western music (which they loved) and keeping the comedy (which baffled them) to a minimum. What frightened us most about the trip was a story about a stand-up comic who was doing his act when a soldier stepped up from the audience and peed all over him. That sort of criticism sounded a little too direct for us.

After a fortnight, we were happy to return to our kind of clubs – a week in Cleethorpes, a week in Leeds at the City Varieties, a week at Greasbrough Social Club (a unique club near Rotherham that put on better bills than the Palladium). On one booking, we were on with Bob Monkhouse, The Seekers and five more acts.

While we were at Greasbrough, we were asked to double at the Kon Tiki in Wakefield. Jackie Trent, who was number one in the charts at the time, had taken ill, so over we went and my opening line was: 'As the management of the Kon Tiki said to Jackie Trent, "Where Are You Now My Love?",' the title of her hit. It went down very well with the audience but not with the management, who had a surprisingly thin skin when it came to humour at their expense.

In September, we did a week of venues around Manchester for an agent called Sonny Gross, a leading contender for world's worst agent. We were to appear at two venues a night and we were looking forward to it: it meant we would be staying at home for a week.

On the Wednesday, Sonny rang to ask if we could do an extra late spot in Salford on the Saturday night and we agreed, as usual. On the Thursday, the secretary from the Co-op Club in Pendleton called and asked what time we would be arriving on Saturday. I explained that on Saturday we were working at the

Carlisle Club in Eccles and the Luxor Club in Hulme. He replied that Sonny had booked us in and we were advertised. I said, 'OK. We'll be there.'

That Friday, we were working at the Station Hotel, Swinton, run by a pal of ours, Johnny Fehan. 'What time will you be here tomorrow?' he asked. An alarming pattern was beginning to emerge.

I replied carefully, 'We are working tomorrow at the Co-op Club, the Carlisle Club, the Luxor Club and a late club in Salford.'

'Well, Sonny has booked you in and you're advertised,' Johnny replied.

So that Saturday night we did the Co-op, the Station, the Carlisle and the Luxor, and we were knackered. Sonny's partner was in the Luxor and he told us that Sonny was in the club in Salford keeping things going until we got there. So we never went, which served him right.

CHAPTER FOUR

Toppermost Of The Poppermost

It sounds callous, and I don't mean to be unkind, but for a time the break-up of my engagement to Pat felt like a blessed release.

I tried to throw myself into the act and we started to earn some decent money, certainly compared to our friends who were doing ordinary jobs, but we got rid of it as fast as it arrived. I invested a lot of money in houses, but unfortunately they were public houses and the money went straight over the bar. It was just earn and spend. We never seemed to have anything to show for it.

My ambition at that time was to have £2,000 in the bank. I thought I would be made for life if I got that but I never even looked like getting anywhere near. Cash just burned a hole in my pocket. It was a fantastic change when we started getting enough money to go out every day of the week. The trouble was we *did* go out every day of the week and we spent it all, but we were young lads with no thoughts for the future.

I was still living at my parents' house: it was just too comfortable at home. In search of independence, I did once get a flat in Moss Side, thinking it was time that I grew up and moved away, but after a week I was back with all my washing. No one looks after you quite like your mother, so I went back home. She always used to spoil me and get in some Blue Riband chocolate biscuits. My sister and brother still tease me about getting that sort of special treatment.

We had regular gigs at two lively Manchester clubs, the Princess and the Domino. We used to follow some big pop acts of the day such as The Springfields and Freddie And The Dreamers, and seemed to do really well. Syd and Eddie went down so well that some of the pop acts did not want to follow us.

My love life brightened up a little as well when I met a girl called Millie and went out with her a couple of times. She was a nice girl but it didn't work out between us and then I met another girl at the Princess Club. I had already seen her in the Wilton, dancing with a mate. I thought her name was Heather but, when I saw her again at the Domino and I plucked up the courage to ask if I could take her out, I found she was called Sandra.

Her full name was Sandra Bigwood. We went out a

few times and got on well, even though she made it clear she was not exactly a fan of showbusiness. We carried on courting and the relationship grew from there. My parents went to meet Sandra's parents and we went through everything our parents had gone through before us. Being in showbusiness at that level, however, just going round the pubs and clubs, seemed like a very strange method of making a living to the normal person. It was a way of life they couldn't really comprehend. We were doing very well, thank you very much, but no one could see that there was any future in it, least of all us.

When I say that Sandra was not exactly a fan of showbusiness, I am not telling the whole story. Sandra hated showbusiness with a passion that I never quite understood, given that it provided a good living. She wasn't too keen on me having been out with Millie either, because they had been mates. She used to criticise Millie for our brief fling. She would often sneer that she had seen poor Millie walking in with my suitbag over her shoulder, strutting her 'I'm going out with a star' stuff, as Sandra used to call it.

In 1964, we did our first summer season in Weymouth with The Hollies, Shane Fenton And The Fentones, and the American Big Dee Irwin, who sang 'Would You Like To Swing On A Star?'.

It was quite a culture shock for Big Dee. While we were in Weymouth, he bought a speedboat and decided to learn how to waterski. The trouble was he was about 20 stone and the boat just wasn't powerful enough to shift him. The kid who was driving the boat fell out, leaving it going round and round in circles. It finished up almost wrecking itself on the beach.

Big Dee wouldn't take a hint, though. He had the boat repaired and tied it up at night. The trouble was he only used about three feet of rope, so when the tide went out the boat was left suspended, and when it came back in it filled with water and sank.

Mind you, we had transport problems before we even got to Weymouth. We'd worked in Yorkshire the night before and the brakes on the Minivan didn't seem too clever. When I went to pick up Syd at about five in the morning, I realised that I had no brakes at all. We called out the AA man, who said the brake pipe was split and told us we couldn't go anywhere until we'd had it fixed. We panicked and decided to drive down there with just a handbrake. The roads weren't so busy then but it was still a nightmare journey. I've never been so relieved as when we went down that final huge hill into Weymouth in first gear with me tugging as hard on the handbrake as I could. We made it, but goodness knows how.

That was the year we thought we'd landed our big break. A Charlie Drake summer season called *Man In The Moon* was pulled from its planned run at the Queen's Theatre in Blackpool. Evidently someone decided they weren't ready for that level of sophistication in the resort at that time. So, in an old-fashioned turn of events, the management decided to switch back to a traditional variety bill.

Our agent at the time was Joe Collins, father of the rather more famous Joan and Jackie. Joe got his right-hand man Cyril Gibbons to give us the call to go into this top variety bill with Sabrina, Reg 'Confidentially' Dixon, the Jones Boys and a couple of other acts. But there was a problem. We needed music for a 12-piece band and we just didn't have any music. Our tunes were all written on the back of cigarette packets. That was quite enough to get us round the clubs. So we got our music written for us by a keyboard player, who unfortunately liked a drink. The result was amateurish to say the least, but what did we know? We were comedians, not musicians.

We didn't even have any proper billing either. We were called Syd and Eddie and that was that. In those days you had to have a witty description like 'the Jeyes Brothers – a fluid act!' Or preferably something genuinely amusing. So, some genius at Blackpool gave us our billing. We were astonished to see on the posters: 'Syd and Eddie – 2 Funny 4 Words'.

The band call was a nightmare. To his credit, the band leader was a very nice man and tried hard to help us sort it out, but the musicians were complete bastards. They really put us through it trying to arrange our music, but it was a foreign language to us. It got worse when we started to go through our act. We did a skit on Freddie And The Dreamers. 'You can't do

Freddie And The Dreamers, the Jones Boys do Freddie And The Dreamers,' we were told firmly.

Oh, all right. 'We do a take-off of Mick Jagger and the Rolling Stones.'

'You can't do that. The Jones Boys do Mick Jagger and the Rolling Stones.'

So the music was wrong and our act was cut to shreds because of what other people were doing. We went on at Blackpool on a Monday night and it was awful. We had two eight-minute spots but we just couldn't hack it. We had never been in a theatre in our lives. The manager was a kind fellow really, but he said, 'I'm sorry, lads, but I've got to pay you off. It's not your fault. I didn't really want an act like yours. I wanted a crosstalk, patter act, and that's not you.'

I was pretty cut up. Nobody likes rejection and I like it less than most people. I was engaged to Sandra by then and I went to see her, in search of some tender loving care I suppose.

'What are you doing here?' she asked.

'We got paid off,' I admitted sadly. The experience had reduced me to tears. Nobody feels rejection like a comic.

'Good,' she said with some relish. 'I'm glad. You were getting too bigheaded.'

That hardly made me feel better and, with hindsight, the danger signals were there loud and clear, but I failed to see them. Sandra really did hate showbusiness and she never made a secret of it.

Relationships in showbusiness are never easy and I confess I was very naive about the ways of the world. Syd and I travelled a lot up to the north-east clubs in those days and we always seemed to have a good time, but I wasn't playing away from home. In fact, I was so innocent I kept showing Sandra lots of pictures of some of the people we met and quite a few of them seemed to be attractive young girls. That's how mad I was but, as I wasn't up to anything, I never thought anything of it. On one pop tour, I even had a picture taken with Syd and two pretty young girls pointing up at a poster with our names on it. And I sent that picture back to Sandra in a letter. How daft can you get?

Even so, Sandra and I were married in September 1965. Now, when it comes to punctuality, I'm a real panicker, and on my wedding day I was obsessive about being early. Looking back it seems ridiculous, but I would rather be two hours early than five minutes late. Sandra and I were getting married at 2pm in Droylsden, about four miles from where I lived. I had arranged for a taxi firm, Plane's Taxis, to come to my house 24 Linwood Street at one o'clock. But at one o'clock the cab was not there. Nobody was remotely worried but me. Why should the cab come an hour early for a 15-minute journey?

Well, *I* thought it should. We didn't have a telephone and I rushed to the phone box on the corner only to be told it was on its way. But, at 1.15, the cab still wasn't there. I flipped. I thought, I'm not having this. And I jumped in my Minivan and drove to the cab office.

'Where's my cab?' I demanded.

'He's just phoned in,' he told me. 'He's at your house. Wait here.'

So the cab came for me there and I had to get one of my mates to go and pick up the Minivan later from outside the cab shop.

Getting married is one thing. Living happily ever after is quite another. I can remember a few weeks into the marriage it wasn't really working. I was just so used to being with the lads all the time, playing cards or going down the pub or whatever, and suddenly my life was not like that at all. Partly, that had come to a stop because me and Syd were working so hard. But, when we did have the odd Friday night free and I wanted to go out for a laugh with my mates, I would find I was supposed to be tiling the bathroom floor! Or putting wallpaper up. I was 24 when I got married, but looking back it was a very naive and immature 24.

Sandra and I got a house in Chorlton-cum-Hardy, near to the school where I used to go. I had to lie about what I did because they wouldn't give mortgages to entertainers, as it wasn't considered a steady job and there was no wage slip. A mate of mine who had a garage pretended I was a mechanic working for them and that's how I got the mortgage on our first house. That was 228 Manly Road, a semi-detached suburban house.

It was an enormous shock going from the freedom of living at home, with my mum doing everything and waiting on me hand and foot, to being married. I was a husband and in some ways I still felt like a kid. After a few weeks, I couldn't handle it. We went out to a pub in Cheshire for a serious talk because I realised this wasn't what I wanted.

Of course, I was away an awful lot as well, which made our lives much more difficult. Sandra was left at home on her own which was very hard for her as well. I got very stressed, and Sandra and I had to have a real heart to heart. I just wasn't very good at the settled-down domestic bit. The garden was a wilderness and that suited me fine. The neighbour kept telling me how the bloke who lived there before used to grow wonderful roses. It was a none too subtle hint that, naturally, I chose to totally ignore. To me, the neighbours were from another planet. I was never there, so the state of the garden was of no interest to me. Eventually, my father-in-law attacked it all with weedkiller.

I just couldn't handle the whole settling-down bit. It must have been just as hard for Sandra as it was for me. So naturally, as we were unsure about our relationship, we plunged pretty quickly into having a family. Samantha was born 11 months after we got married. She arrived the night England beat Portugal in the 1966 World Cup.

Sandra had to stay in hospital because Sammy was

premature. She was still in hospital on the Saturday when England played Germany in the Final. I sat by the bedside listening to the match, trying to be a caring husband, but I kept hearing snatches of the match from a radio and, with people cheering and shouting as the game went on, it was very distracting. I am not proud of myself but Sandra was pretty out of it and, at half-time, I just had to leave her to it and go and watch the second half of the World Cup Final. Alison was born four years afterwards during the Mexico World Cup. I used to joke that it was a good job we didn't qualify for the next two World Cups as having two daughters was just right.

I didn't settle down because we started to travel further away and we were constantly working all of the time. Sandra often mentioned she didn't like showbusiness, and subsequently she didn't like me. It's a difficult business to stay faithful in. Quasimodo could pull if he was in showbiz.

The following Sunday, we were paying our first visit to South Wales to do a week at Cleopatra's Club in Cardiff. The owner was a Welsh Egyptian called Annis Abraham and topping the bill was a Jewish comedian called Ray Martine. We were expecting sparks to fly when on the first night we were sitting with Annis watching Ray. He was struggling a little, but slowly they were warming to him and he came to the part of his act where he read an emotional letter from his mother. He had quite a search before he found the letter but it went down very well when he did. Annis turned to us and said, 'It's a good job he found that letter, otherwise he would have died a death!' Somehow, Ray managed to find that vital letter every night so all was well.

The characters we met in those days were quite something. There was an old guy called Frank who did an act dressed as a tramp. He had a routine where the compere would come out and apologise that the first act had not turned up. Frank would wander on and offer to do a song, quickly get the audience on his side and then go into his act. He had once appeared at a South Shields complex where three clubs all backed on to each other. After finishing one act, he went out the back door of the club but was stopped by the doorman at the next one, who wouldn't let him in. He tried to explain he was the turn but then he realised he was in the wrong club and he rushed to the right club where the compere was frantically ad-libbing.

Frank finally abandoned his act after a disastrous night in Manchester. He had gone out of the back door and was peering through a gap in the curtains, waiting for his cue to go on, when a policeman tapped him on the shoulder and took him down to the station for acting suspiciously.

Some of the clubs were hardly in the business of providing family entertainment. We did regular gigs at the College Club where, as I mentioned before, we always went well after all the bluer acts. The owner Les

Lawrence always wanted something different. One night, a young stripper called Rose Marie was there. She was only about 19 and very attractive, so not surprisingly she was quite popular. In the second half, they had another stripper, a girl called Kinky Minky, from London. She went on. Then there was a comic and, in the second half, Rose Marie came on again followed by Kinky Minky. And they started doing a lesbian act that was alarmingly explicit.

There was total shocked silence in the club, because this was back in the 1960s when people still thought lesbians lived on a Greek Island. Even today it would be quite shocking. And it was against the law. In the end, the compere had to pull one of the girls' legs to stop them.

Afterwards, there was a piece in the paper about how disgusting the stag show at the College Club had been. And the reporter had left before the lesbian act! So what he would have thought if he'd stayed, who knows.

The following week we did the same show and the place was full of coppers. Les didn't care a damn, he just wanted to keep the punters coming in. One night, the keeper from Belle Vue Zoo was in and Les asked him to bring in two lions to sit on the stage and watch the stripper in action.

'That's not possible, Mr Lawrence,' said the keeper politely.

'What do you mean it's not possible?' shouted Les. 'It's a sensational idea.'

'Mr Lawrence,' the keeper said patiently, 'what do you think we keep them in cages for?'

It was a laugh a minute travelling the country with Syd and his brother Dave, who became our road manager in spite of his lack of somewhat basic qualifications – he couldn't drive. But Dave was a great, good-natured guy who was excellent at helping with the gear and I liked driving myself so it was no problem. My memories of those amazing days are mainly of laughter, both on and off stage. I used to say we were the luckiest guys alive. Who else has a job where you get paid to spend the day laughing?

Dave remains one of my greatest friends to this day. He is a terrific bloke for a comedian to have by his side because he has a wonderful way of grabbing hold of the wrong end of the stick and clinging on with both hands. And he never minds laughing at himself, so long as it's done in the spirit of friendship.

Dave has brightened up many long trips across Britain with his knack for choosing the slightly wrong word. After a while, we developed our own private language. Being hungry as usual, I said to Dave on one trip as a joke, 'Shall we stop and have something to eat at the Little Chief?' Dave took everything I said as gospel and we always called them Little Chiefs after that. It made them sound so much more interesting than Little Chefs.

Dave really enjoyed any new use of language. An old

actor called Bertie Hare once came to see us in panto at Bristol. He met up with Dave and in his very distinguished, upper-crust voice said, 'I see you're still a bit of room at the front, Dave.'

'You what?' asked Dave, completely baffled.

'Rhymes with room at the front, begins with c...'

I prompted him and the penny dropped.

'That's brilliant,' said Dave who loves rhyming slang. 'I'm having that.'

Some time later, one of Dave's mates came in and he did his infamous chuckle and said, 'You're a bit of a front room, aren't you?' So that went straight into our language. Anyone we don't like, he's a bit of a front room.

When I was in Nottingham, I was on low-calorie lager for my health. All of a sudden the call rang out, 'Eddie Large on stage.' I necked back my drink and ran on.

A bit later that night Dave came up and warned me gravely. 'Hey, you shouldn't be drinking that stuff as fast as that, Eddie,' said Dave with real concern in his voice. 'You'll be going on stage abbreviated.' So naturally now, in our language, abbreviated means drunk.

We used to have a musical director and piano player called Brian Pendleton, who was never really quite on our wavelength. He was well spoken, a toffee-nosed kind of guy who always seemed to think he was a cut above everyone else. Dave and Brian were like oil and water, and they just never got on. Dave called him

Pengy, which he loathed. 'Call me Brian,' Pendleton would say.

'All right, Pengy,' Dave would reply in his typically Manc manner.

It was hardly a match made in heaven, but the verbal conflict brightened many a dull cross-country trip.

Once we were driving from Manchester to Croydon. I was at the wheel because, although Dave did pass his test after three years in the job, he very rarely drove. We were on our way to the Fairfield Hall and we were playing our own version of *Name That Tune* where you were given the first word of the answer to start with. If the first word was 'My' you'd be guessing 'My Way', 'My Generation' and so on until you got the right answer.

Dave was never desperately successful at this game and, with his musical background, Brian was getting all the answers right, which was getting right up Dave's nose. Dave kept saying, 'Not my era, not my era' in his frustration.

At the time, Nottingham Forest had a record in the charts called 'We've Got The Whole World In Our Hands'. On my turn, the others had got 'We've Got The...' but then they were stuck. To help the process along I said, 'The next word starts with W.'

'I've got it,' cried Syd. '"We've Got The Whole World In Our Hands".'

'Correct,' I said, deeply relieved that we could move on at last.

'****ing W,' moans Dave.

We thought for a second and then I said, 'Sorry, Dave, I meant H.'

'No wonder I can't win at this game,' he yelled and we just fell about.

In the early 1970s, we went up to the north-east and it was crazy every night, everybody going absolutely berserk doing daft games. We went on about 11pm and we really struggled. The audience was paralytic and in no state to listen to two comedians.

When we came off the compere seemed pleased. 'That was good, you did well,' he said. Next night it was a stag night. They had about eight strippers on, and then me and Syd. We died a death. The compere said afterwards, 'You did well, you know. For a Tuesday.' Wednesday night was bier keller night so they all wanted to sing drinking songs. The place was like a lake with beer, absolute chaos. But again the compere was happy.

We said, 'What are you talking about, we just died.'

'No, lads,' he said, 'you've done well. But Thursday, Friday and Saturday are really difficult nights.'

Wales is a world of its own. When VAT came in we never used to get it at first because no one knew what it was all about. It became complicated so I went to see the VAT man and learned all about the new tax because I knew we would have to pay, and get paid, VAT. So off we went armed with a receipt book to play a club in the valleys of Wales. I got my cheque and of course there was no VAT included. I tackled the club secretary and asked, 'What about our VAT?'

'VAT, boyo?' he said. 'We haven't gone decimal up here yet.'

It was a tough world but I was never bothered about that. I had a pretty tough upbringing. As a teenager, I was always getting in fights and I could handle myself. I wasn't frightened of a few pompous club owners. People always used to say that if you can work Manchester you can work anywhere. But, when I go to some of these places and see the wrecked cars and the broken glasses outside, I wonder at the things I used to put myself through. You need someone to turn to when the abuse is flying. I think that is why a lot of comics turn to drink and become broken men because it's hard to withstand that sort of pressure on your own. We always had each other.

When the 1960s first began to swing, we hardly noticed because we were too busy trying to be funny. We were both music mad, however, and were delighted when we suddenly acquired a whole new string to our bow – comperes on the new pop tours sweeping up and down the country. It was fabulous to be offered a pop tour. I think it was because we were the same age as a lot of the groups.

We couldn't handle the 'screamagers' at first. They knew who was coming on next and they didn't want to listen to anyone else. We worked out a gag for Syd to slowly come and join me on stage because there was too much screaming to listen to our normal act. But it was great experience.

Our pop career started with a crisis, however.

We were in Glasgow at the Odeon and I was chuffed to be working back in the city I was born in. Dionne Warwick was the star of the tour and unfortunately her big arrival was marred when she got out of the coach and forgot that the traffic goes the opposite way over here and was just clipped by a bus on the side of her leg. I don't think she was ever too happy on the tour in the first place but this accident really put the cat among the pigeons.

She was taken off to hospital and Ron the tour manager briefed me. 'I want you to say, "We've got some bad news and some good news – the bad news is that Dionne Warwick has been involved in an unfortunate accident and she can't perform for you tonight. The good news is that The Searchers have agreed to do a greatly extended spot."'

I stood up at the first house to make this tortuous announcement and there was a round of groans after I told the audience that Dionne would not be appearing, but there were cheers when I gave them the information about The Searchers. At the second house, though, there was almost a revolution. I only got the first half of the announcement out and the place was in uproar. They were a Scottish crowd convinced the English were cheating them yet again.

We couldn't get out of the place for about an hour as

they just wouldn't calm down. I tried to get round them by insisting I was born in Glasgow but I don't think they believed me.

We had more trouble in Colchester. The Searchers' return flight from a Paris gig was delayed and they weren't going to make the first house. The manager said, 'Go on and say, "Due to a flight delay beyond our control The Searchers will not be appearing in the first house."'

I did as I was told. Unfortunately, the audience thought it was a joke and they just laughed. I kept trying to say it was serious and The Searchers really weren't coming and they kept laughing. Until they discovered I really *was* serious and went crazy.

The Isley Brothers were a great musical group but they were always late. After a few rows about timekeeping the tour manager said, 'If you're not here on time, we're leaving without you.' The coach used to park just behind Baker Street near Allsop Place, the starting point for pop tours in the 1960s (which inspired the opening lines of Gerry Rafferty's 'Baker Street'). The Isley Brothers had kept us waiting yet again so the tour manager said, 'Right, we've given those guys enough warnings. We're not waiting any longer. Off we go.'

The coach pulled out of Allsop Place when the Isley Brothers were just coming around the corner in a cab. They jumped out of the cab but the coach didn't stop. The tour manager had had just about enough. So the

Isley Brothers jumped back in the cab and said, 'ABC Chester, man.'

The cabbie was pretty surprised but he set straight off for the north. The Brothers never thought it could be so far but it was quite a fare.

Pop drummers are often a little odd. The Alan Elsdon Band had a drummer who would go completely mad at the start of every tour, a total loony tune. He would go out and get completely plastered and do loads of daft things. Then, two days before the tour finished, he wouldn't drink because he was going back to his wife and wanted it to seem like he had been well behaved and sober. This was the Gene Pitney tour with Peter and Gordon, Lulu and the Luvvers, and The Zombies. Peter and Gordon were much too clever to be in showbiz but were still nice lads.

Because they were bored on the tour, these guys developed a bizarre competition. They used to spend their time building little robots that would fight. They had these little mechanical monsters that would scrap and the pop guys would be standing in the background cheering. It was a bit strange but touring can be boring and you need some distractions.

Gordon Waller and Peter Asher were slightly out of place with the rest of us because they were posh public schoolboys; nice enough if a little toffee-nosed. Gordon was a bit off the wall as well. We all had small robots and he came in with a huge robot and up until then the drummer's much smaller robot had been the champion. So instantly everyone started feeling sorry for the drummer, as they thought he was going to get beaten at last. We thought it was a little unsporting. But the match went on and, just as they squared up to each other, the drummer poured lighter fuel all over Gordon's robot and set fire to it. The big robot burst into flames and bits of it started melting. Waller's face was a picture! He couldn't believe what he was seeing. His magnificent would-be champion robot was destroyed before his very eyes. The place was in total uproar and it was a very popular outcome. Gordon had really spent some cash on his robot.

It was on this tour that we came close to showbusiness greatness. Or at least Syd's guitar did. At the Adelphi in Slough, we shared a dressing room with Peter and Gordon. We had arrived early so I was having a shave and Syd was strumming his guitar when in walked this scruffy-looking bloke who asked where Peter Asher was. We explained Peter hadn't arrived yet and told the stranger he could wait.

We could tell by his accent that he was from Liverpool and, a moment or so later, we both realised this was Paul McCartney. This was 16 November 1965 and The Beatles were the biggest group there had ever been. Syd and I were massive fans, along with the rest of the country, but when confronted by one of our heroes we were tongue-tied beyond belief. When Peter arrived, he asked Paul to play some songs from the album they were working on and Paul borrowed Syd's guitar to play 'Norwegian Wood', 'Day Tripper' and a few others. He even asked us what we thought. We couldn't believe it. Paul introduced us in the second show from an offstage mike and, even though he called us Syd and Edie, I couldn't care less. And Syd will never part with his guitar.

On the same tour, we got to the Liverpool Empire on the Sunday night. We did the theatres on a Sunday night and the cinemas in the week. When we arrived, there was an officious guy telling us that Syd and Eddie wouldn't be working here tonight. Evidently, there was some bizarre bylaw that banned pairs of actors who used crosstalk or props. We were devastated. We had to explain to the stage manager that we didn't actually do any crosstalk, just me telling jokes against Syd, so they let us go on in the end. It was a peculiar place the Liverpool Empire because they were very militant. Clive Lea of The Rockin' Berries, who was also an impressionist, had to get special permission to use his Norman Wisdom cap!

Occasionally, reality did thrust its way into our strange world. One night, when we got back to Syd's house in the early hours from the Greasbrough Social, all the lights were on. Syd's eldest brother Peter came rushing out and said, 'Me dad's dead.'

Syd was devastated, obviously. I felt awful. I wanted to do something to help but I couldn't think of anything.

Syd's dad Cyril was a top-notch fellow. He was just 50 years of age, and a real character, a funny, funny man.

I really liked him but I felt like a spare part so I just went home on my own. I was stunned, so I don't know how Syd and his family must have felt to lose someone so early in life. I went round the next day and felt I didn't have the words to say, but I surprised myself when I talked to Syd's poor mother Gladys about her loss. The funeral was just awful.

The pop tours were a very educational time of my life. It was the first time I had ever seen farts lit, on an overnight trip across the country. Of course, everyone on board had been drinking heavily, including me. But the first time I saw flames shoot across the bus out of someone's backside it sobered me up almost instantly. Then, of course, someone had to take his trousers off and naturally the flames burned the hairs round his bum, which produced great hilarity.

It was also our first experience of groupies, who were absolutely determined to get to grips with the pop singers and sadly not remotely interested in a pair of Manchester comedians. We couldn't pull any groupies but at least they touched us occasionally. They used to pull our hair when they got out of the coach.

In Cardiff, one of the lads from a band slipped a groupie into the theatre for fairly obvious reasons.

We had learned on the previous tour that you couldn't tell jokes because the kids were screaming all the time. So I would do an offstage announcement and then go on and say, 'I'm looking for my mate Syd. Has anybody seen him?'

Then Syd would come walking slowly on from the other side of the stage and by the time he got to me the pop fans were screaming so loud for the next act that we just had to get off. But with one tour under our belt we were a bit more confident now, cocky even, and in Cardiff I was doing the routine about having lost Syd. When he should have come on, there was no sign of him. I was getting a bit desperate because the audience was getting louder and I just wanted to finish the gag and get off. But there was no sign of Syd. Sweat was pouring off me and I had to introduce the next act without him.

I was furious. A few minutes later Syd rushed up all hot and bothered. 'I'm sorry about that.'

'**** off,' I said.

He knew he was in the wrong and he confessed that he had been upstairs shagging this groupie and he got so carried away he forgot all about our compering.

It was an exciting world but, while we both loved pop music, we weren't really part of it. We were northern comics just brought along to be the comperes.

Maybe I'm biased, but in showbusiness I don't think it comes much tougher than playing the clubs. If music-hall people had a difficult time with their audience, they used to leave quietly by the stage door, while sometimes we had to walk out right through the unhappy punters afterwards. And we did have to make some difficult exits.

The Hilton Castle Club in the north-east lives in my

memory as a night to forget. We did a noon and night as they used to call it. All the lads used to come in at lunchtime and, if they liked you, they would come back in at night with their wives. At lunchtime, they were all in there reading the Sunday papers while we were battling to be hilarious, but we just gave it our best shot as usual. We must have done all right because that night the place was packed.

All the time in those early days, we were fighting to do just two spots. The working men's clubs wanted you to do three or four spots, and that meant five if we went on to do a nightclub afterwards. At the Hilton Castle, we had left all our gear. When we turned up for the evening, I asked hopefully, 'Is there anyone on with us tonight?'

'No,' came the cheerless and uncompromising reply from the concert secretary.

'How many spots are we doing?' I enquired tentatively.

'Oh three, maybe four,' was the confident response.

'No, no, no,' I said. 'We have an agreement with the agent that we only do two spots.'

'No, bonny lad,' said the secretary. 'You'll do three tonight.'

So the argument was on. Syd and I were totally united on this but somehow I was always in the firing line. Syd was in hiding at this point. It was always me who had to go and get the money and negotiate the conditions. Syd is allergic to confrontation. The concert secretary, meanwhile, went for reinforcements. And they got me in this little committee room and then the inquisition began.

The central line of enquiry seemed to be: 'Do you know how many ****ing hours I have to work down the ****ing pit to earn the money we're paying you for telling a few jokes?'

They pushed me up against the wall and really had a go, but I've got this very Scottish stubbornness in me and I never could back down. The easy way out would have been for me to say, 'Oh, all right then, we'll do three spots.' But we had been fighting for proper conditions for ages and I am not good at backing down when I believe I'm right.

'All we're gonna do is the two spots we agreed,' I kept insisting. 'You can't follow yourself in our business. It just doesn't work.'

The secretary was quite a nice fellow, to be honest, and after a while he was trying to talk the others into agreeing with me, but the rest of the committee were adamant. And of course it's going round the club that these two guys are not going to do what's expected. So I said to Syd, 'Get the gear, we're going.'

Syd went on stage to retrieve our gear and they were all throwing beer mats at him and the odd bottle. Luckily, there was a back door that time. If there wasn't, I don't think we would have got out alive.

The agent who booked us was a guy called Jimmy Dunn (who had such a masterful showbusiness brain that, when he was once asked for a strong act for a

Sunday lunchtime stag do, he sent in a noted muscleman). I said, 'Jimmy, we had an agreement to do two half-hour spots.'

He said, 'Yeah, but I thought you could do three of 20 minutes instead.'

'Jimmy,' I groaned, 'it doesn't work like that.'

We had lots of hassles with concert secretaries in those days. We went to one club and told them we had to be away by ten o'clock.

'Ten, bonny lad?' came the inevitable reply. 'You'll still be on stage then.'

'We've got an agreement with the agent.'

'We know nothing aboot it.'

Oh no, here we go again, I thought but I insisted. I tried to explain, 'Look, we have to do this nightclub at Chester le Street later, but we'll do you two half-hour spots before ten o'clock.'

'All right,' he said thoughtfully, and then went on stage with the microphone and announced, 'Here is Syd and Eddie. They're going to do two half-hour spots because they've got to be away to a nightclub in Chester le Street. Now, I know nothing about this. As far as I'm concerned, we're paying them to be here all night. Anyway, here they are, Syd and Eddie.'

Now, you go on stage and entertain an audience of hard-working, laughter-starved Geordies who have just been told that you are short-changing them. It did not go well. They all hated us but we had to go through the act with our smiles fixed in place. It was purgatory.

Pantomime always produces surprise laughs. In *Cinderella*, the little white ponies who pulled the coach appeared to have a nervous problem that led them to deposit large dollops of dung on the stage. That often produced some of the biggest laughs of the night.

Panto wasn't easy. We were the broker's men and we were landed with corny scripts: 'Here is a writ and we're the men who writ it.' We knew it was the sort of stuff the ponies left. We were in our twenties and this old stuff had been around for years, but we had to do at least some of it, though we tried to bring it up to date where we could. But we weren't a conventional double act. People used to criticise us for not being 50–50 on stage. They said we were more 80–20 in what we did on stage with me doing the lion's share and it should be split more equally. Why? There are no rules in making people laugh. If it works, do it. I never sat down and plotted to grab the limelight. The way we performed just evolved naturally.

In those days, there was a lot of travelling involved and acts were always trying to think of ways to keep the expenses down. Some would trail caravans round and one singing duo decided to get a camper van. One of the beds was above the driver's seat and had a window on the side. After a long trip up to the north-east, they arrived in the early hours. It was really foggy, so they just found somewhere to park and crashed out. Later in the morning, they were woken by laughter and discovered to their embarrassment that one of them had gone to sleep with no clothes on and his bottom pressed against the curtainless window. They had parked in a bus stop.

After the panto, we worked in and around Manchester almost every night. It's amazing how many live venues there were for comedy compared to today. But our bid for world domination eventually led us to Malta for three weeks. For the first three days we worked at a theatre in Valetta, with Helen Shapiro topping the bill, and then for the rest of the time at a hotel in St Andrews. We did a lot of visual stuff in the act so it went down well with the Maltese. We used to do Speedy Gonzales where I used to run around the audience dressed in a poncho and wearing a big sombrero.

Syd and I were always good friends but we did have our own private lives. We never really discussed it but there was a sort of unspoken agreement that we didn't want to live in each other's pocket. Syd had to get married in 1967. His bride, Mavis, was nice but she was also a very young girl, and only a teenager when she had their first child, Paul.

She had been with Syd since she was 15. I feel sorry for her in a lot of ways. She had a lot on but at the time we didn't realise that Paul was hyperactive. Paul was always the kid who would turn the tap on behind the bar and try and drown the cat. He was like Dennis the Menace, but worse. She had all that to put up with being so young and having a boy who was a bit lively to say the least. Syd's marriage to Mavis came under the same sort of long-distance strain that mine and Sandra's experienced. Neither of us was a saint, and neither of us went home as often as most husbands seemed to manage.

Syd was well into his affair with dancer Sheree when an early tragedy struck. We were at the London Palladium in 1971 on the Cliff Richard show. I was staying with a pal and his wife in Croydon when I got a call from Sandra to say that Paul had had a bad accident. He'd run out into the road and a milk float had hit him and the bottom part of his leg was ripped off. Mavis had to pick up the severed leg in a towel. It must have been terrible for her. She didn't know where Syd was so she got Sandra to telephone me. 'Get Syd to contact Mavis. Quick!'

I didn't know where he was. There were no mobile phones in those days, so I drove into the Palladium, desperately hoping Syd would be in early, and met Sheree's formidable mother. She said he was out shopping with Sheree. I told her of the emergency and she said, 'Don't you tell him, I'll tell him.'

I thought, Flippin' heck, missus, you've only known him five minutes, we've been together for years. But it was not a pleasant thing to tell someone and I wasn't actually looking forward to it. He still had to do the show. I couldn't believe Mavis didn't know how to contact him. I'm not trying to hold myself up as anything special but I always rang my kids every day. I still do even though they're in their thirties.

When we finished at the Palladium, we went to see Paul in hospital, where he'd had his leg stitched back on. I said, 'How are you doing, Paul?' and he strained to kick me with his bad leg. That's what he was like, Paul – difficult, a nightmare for a young girl like Mavis to look after. He used to put her and his sister Donna through hell.

His leg was reattached, which was pretty amazing, but it looked awful. In fact, it looked like a side of bacon because it was so red and the kids at school used to call him 'bacon legs'. When he got a bit older, he was into CB radio and his call sign was Moroccan Black.

That wasn't the only emergency Syd and I shared in those hectic days. We had a terrible car crash in Sunderland. Syd ended up in hospital for two nights and I had to do the act on my own. We used to double in the north-east, do two spots in a working men's club and then a nightclub. We were going from Middlesbrough to Newcastle to appear at midnight, and the crash happened in Sunderland. Syd was driving in his new Ford Corsair and it was our right of way but this other driver didn't stop and smashed right into us.

I ducked down and there was a horrible smash. I was all right and jumped out and had a go at this other driver. Then I heard this plaintive voice shout 'Eddie' from behind me and realised Syd was trapped in the car. A light switch had gone right through his knee, and the car was on fire. That very day we had spent £500 on a new PA system that was in the car, and I'm thinking that I've got to get that PA system out, as I can't have £500 going up in smoke. The fire brigade came and put the fire out and everything was all right, but I was still more concerned about our new gear than about Syd I'm afraid.

Syd had to go to hospital and the other driver was whisked away. His mates were passing, saw how drunk he was and took him off. A copper told us later that he got let off.

Syd went back home to Manchester. There was one night to go and I did the working men's club on my own. I did OK, amazingly enough, and the second spot went even better. I went home that night and saw Syd the next day. He was in bed and I counted the money out for him, which he has never forgotten. I bored him to tears for an hour or two telling him how well it went just to keep him on the back foot.

The car was a write-off. We were both very lucky.

As we started to make a better living, I was able to spend a bit more time on the golf course. I was delighted to play at Chorlton Golf Club from time to time with Joe Mercer, the manager of my beloved Manchester City. We both lived in Chorlton-cum-Hardy and Joe was a lovely guy. I was always very proud to play with him.

In 1970, City reached the League Cup Final at Wembley and beat West Bromwich Albion 2–1. Francis Lee had one of his best ever games for City. I went with two of my mates, Fred Evans and Johnny Tye. We went back to the hotel afterwards because I knew a few of the players. Joe came straight up to the three of us with the gleaming trophy itself and said, 'There, Eddie. I'll play you for that at Chorlton.' My mates have never forgotten it. Joe was a wonderful guy, even if he was only joking.

CHAPTER FIVE

Opportunity Knocks

Hughie Green's long-running television talent show Opportunity Knocks was a well-trodden route to stardom, but for a long time I was convinced it was not one we ought to take. In our youthful naivety, we thought we were too good for it.

We were doing a storm on the clubs. We had seen some of our mates, who were good comics, go on *Opportunity Knocks* and do their three minutes and look absolutely hopeless and hideously out of place at seven o'clock on a Monday night. They might have been great in clubs, with all their life and atmosphere, but a television studio left them looking awkward and exposed.

We realised that comics very rarely won *Opportunity Knocks*. Even Su Pollard was beaten by a singing duck, so we didn't really want to be on TV's big talent show, thank you very much.

But we had an eccentric manager, Brian Hart – better known as the Major – who persuaded us to go on. He was fresh out of the army and he fancied himself as a showbiz agent. He was clueless but full of enthusiasm, and he pushed and pushed and pushed until we gave in. Once we had put our career in his hands, he plotted our rise to fame and fortune like a military operation. The only problem was that I had a sneaking feeling it was The Retreat from Moscow. But to his everlasting credit Brian talked us into going on *Opportunity Knocks*.

That was a problem, though: our name was honest enough for the northern clubs but we knew we needed something better. After mulling it over for years, we decided on a name change when we went down to Lewes, Sussex, to do a gig at an inn run by a real southern smoothie who was very outspoken. We really did well and he said, 'Here, this ****in' name Syd and Eddie? What sort of name is that?'

The guy was deeply irritating, but unfortunately I knew he was also absolutely right.

We insisted we were very well known in the north. But the bighead from Lewes said, 'You ain't in the ****ing north now.' It was impossible to fault him on that observation either.

A few days later, after mulling the idea over, we were in Sunderland and I went out and bought an old typewriter in a second-hand shop for £8. I spent all night typing all these names. I tried names inspired by soccer players (from Manchester City, of course) like Syd Bell and Eddie Lee. Then I thought I could copy Morecambe and Wise and I thought of Syd Blackpool and Eddie Daft, but no one can copy Morecambe and Wise.

And then, all of a sudden, it just came out – Little and Large. It was like a bolt from the blue. I typed all these names out for some input from my partner, but I typed Little and Large in red. Next day I showed the list to Syd and quick as a flash he picked out Little and Large and said, 'That one,' so he always says it was his idea. In the event, we were both right.

People were reluctant to accept it at first. Some club owners said, 'You're not Little and Large, you're Syd and Eddie in my club.' But gradually they had to accept it and it stuck.

Opportunity Knocks' producer, Royston Mayoh, had seen us as Syd and Eddie years before on a bad night at the Yew Tree in Manchester. His considered professional opinion of us at the time was that we were crap. 'Absolute rubbish' was how he described us.

The Major persuaded him to take another look. Being a proud and fundamentally awkward sort of chap, I pompously said we would not do an audition for anyone, insisting, 'We don't audition for anybody because we are Syd and Eddie.' I still wasn't convinced that we should be appearing on a talent show, even if it was on television.

Brian talked Roy into coming to take another look at our act at a club in Liverpool and, to make it like a proper audition, he brought some of the production team with him. Roy came in with associate producer Len Martin and Doris Barry, who was Hughie Green's assistant. The club was the Wooky Hollow cabaret, and we just stormed the place. Roy came up afterwards and said, 'I can't believe this is the Syd and Eddie I saw at the Yew Tree. You were fantastic. You're on the show.'

Roy started talking straight away about which show we might appear on. We were about to go and do a summer season in Guernsey, so wanted to get on and do our first proper telly as soon as possible.

We had been on the box before but we never used to talk about it because it was a bit insignificant. It was a programme called *Little Big Time*, with Freddie And The Dreamers, back in 1969. We knew the lads in The Dreamers and one of them, a guitarist called Brian Quinn, fancied himself as a bit of an agent. He booked us on to this children's television programme down in Southampton and we did 'Rubber Ball', with me bouncing around the stage like a maniac. We only did about three minutes and it was terrible, but at the time we were excited about doing our first television.

With two more precious years of hard-earned experience, we went on the third programme of *Opportunity Knocks*, quietly confident because we'd been doing clubs and making a good living. But we were also very keen and very determined to do well. We travelled through the night from a show in Hull to get to the Thames studios in time, and slept in the studios overnight. We arrived early in the morning and just bedded down in the dressing room against all the safety rules I'm sure, but Roy Mayoh had alerted the security men to let us in. We were young then, and we didn't care about all that.

The first show we recorded was on a Saturday. We had to rehearse without an audience first, though, and I was hopeless at that. There was no one to bounce off and I hated it. It took me years to be able to feel relaxed trying to get laughs in an empty studio. I couldn't handle it at all. I was desperate to introduce a catchphrase and the big song of the moment was 'In The Summertime', so I kept singing snatches of it but it doesn't really work in a three-minute spot and everyone else was much better than us.

There was a group of Geordie lads on called The Georgians who had won the week before so they were back, and they were very professional. There were three Welsh lads who sang close harmony, and they were even better. There was also a very fine harmonica act and, in the end, we just thought if we come fifth we'll have done very well. Everyone seemed to blow us away.

But, when we got out on the stage and there was a live audience, it was a different ball game. All of a sudden, from feeling out of contention we were suddenly in our element. Even though we only had three minutes, we managed to make an impact. We got 77 on the Clapometer and we were over the moon.

Afterwards, we drove back home to Manchester and I went to a club in Failsworth, The Broadway, where Lovelace Watkins was appearing. He was fantastic in cabaret, as corny and cheesy as you like but a truly great entertainer. He sang all the evocative old songs that other singers had left behind years ago. He was even singing 'Hey Jude', and we'd stopped singing that in 1968. A mate of mine called John Dunkerley got me in to see Lovelace.

Now, Syd and I were very well known at the Broadway because we're local lads. Lovelace was getting into his routine while I was busy getting a few pints down me. He went into 'Hey Jude', and then announced, 'I'd like to invite someone up to help me sing "Hey Jude".' He looked at me and said, 'The big guy, over there...'

I was shocked. But I'd had a few pints so I thought, Why not? Everyone was looking because they could see it's Eddie from Syd and Eddie. Lovelace looked around as if there was something he'd missed.

'What's your name?'

'Eddie.'

'OK, Eddie, let's sing "Hey Jude".'

We got to the 'Na na na' bit, and I had the mike and I was clowning around singing it all out of tune. The audience was laughing because there was only one person in that club who didn't know me, and it was Lovelace Watkins. I screeched, 'Na na na.'

So he went and sat down where I was sitting originally, and my friend John told him quietly, 'That's Eddie from Syd and Eddie. They've just won *Opportunity Knocks* on television tonight.'

Lovelace got back on stage and gave me a squeeze that almost forced the life out of me, gritted his teeth and said, 'I've just heard that Eddie's won *Opportunity Knocks* tonight. Congratulations, Eddie,' and he sat me down very quickly.

When the viewers' votes were counted, we had indeed won *Opportunity Knocks*. People forget with the passing of time, but we only actually won it once. The following week it was Easter and a singer with a religious song just wiped us out. We got a call to say, 'Gwynneth Fleetwood has won it and you've come second.' What a shame, we thought, but she was a lovely singer and we had had our three minutes of glory.

Then at nine o'clock on Saturday morning the phone rang and it was a seriously rattled Roy Mayoh: 'Can you get down here as quick as you can? Gwynneth has got tonsillitis.'

So we rushed down to London totally unprepared. We couldn't decide what to do. We stopped at the motorway services in the days before mobile phones and rang the studio.

'Can we have a piano?'

'OK, we'll get it organised.'

Then we decided we didn't fancy that piano bit and at the next services telephoned to say, 'Roy, forget the piano.'

In the end, we did three minutes that we'd worked out going down the M1. We were shaking like leaves with nerves. So we did it and Hughie Green said, 'Fellas, what are you doing?' We thought we were in big trouble then because Hughie Green was like God to that show. 'What about "In The Summertime"?'

We hadn't done our song take-off so we put it in at the end. We didn't win the second week but shortly after there was an all-winners show and we were on that. We didn't win that either but it still seemed as if we were on week after week.

Apart from in the studio the closest we got to Hughie was after we flew down from the north-east for the all-winners show. He was taking an eight-seater plane up to Tyne Tees to do *The Sky's The Limit*, so he could fly us back in time for a midnight show at a working men's club in Sunderland. We were flying out of Thames at six o'clock and I thought I'd be back in time to watch *Match Of The Day*. Football was all I could think about even in those days.

We got in the plane and off we went, but there was some agitated conversation and we had to land at Birmingham. Oh shit, I thought. So we got off and Hughie was getting involved in an even more animated conversation. There was evidently some fault with the plane. This fellow with a strong Brummie accent came up and insisted we went in the workers' club while they fixed the plane. So we went up there. But they couldn't find what the fault was and this guy was pestering us to go and have a drink. Hughie didn't want a drink and he was getting more and more annoyed.

Then I spotted another man dragging this little kid, who couldn't be more than four or five, up to meet Hughie Green. 'Come on, get Hughie's autograph,' he said. I could see trouble approaching and tried to head it off by offering the guy my autograph. 'Who are you?' he asks. Good question. This particular fan was not about to be deflected an inch. Hughie was his target but he was locked in a deep and complex conversation with this engineer.

'Excuse me, Hughie,' said the man, 'can we have your autograph?'

Hughie exploded. 'Do you mind. I'm in serious conversation here. My aircraft has a problem and I have to get these people up to Newcastle.'

And this little Brummie hits back with the classic line, 'I always knew you were an awkward sod.'

To be fair to Hughie, anyone would have blown, but I daresay that bloke went right round Birmingham badmouthing Hughie for years. But he was OK with us. He was a businessman, really. But he still found time for including brass bands on the show and all those messages of patriotism. You couldn't do it now in these cynical times.

Life was something of an anti-climax after *Opportunity Knocks*. We were recognised in the street and pointed at in the pub occasionally but nothing major in our lives changed and we just went back to the clubs. It was as if this was our 15 minutes of fame and now it was over. The name attracted a lot of attention, like Cannon and Ball, but we were still doing the same clubs for a bit more money. Not much more, but a bit.

Then we were offered a regular spot on the long-running BBC children's show *Crackerjack* in December of 1971. We started doing that early in 1972 and thought this was a brave new dawn for us. In fact, it nearly killed our act stone dead.

We did a season of *Crackerjack* the year after we won *Opportunity Knocks* and our agreed verdict was that we absolutely hated almost every minute. Children were like an unknown species to us. We had never entertained them before in our lives. We could entertain people in clubs, but they most definitely were not children. We said 'Yes' to the job because it was the only television offer we had. We were still managed by the Major, who would have had us doing anything. He'd happily have put us on *Songs Of Praise* if he could have swung it. There was no thought or planning, just get us on. And, to our shame and regret, Syd and I went along with it.

We were on in the days of Michael Aspel hosting the show. *Crackerjack* was returning to the screen after being given a rest by the BBC. Michael was the easy-going presenter and there were all sorts of other people in an intriguing line-up. A young singer called Elaine Paige used to appear – she was so talented that even then you could see she had it all – and a young actor called Stuart Sherwin. And then there was a glamour girl called Heather Barber who always wanted to look good.

To be honest, we hated a lot of the kids' stuff we were doing but we did it as best we could. We'd finish in the studio and then rush off all over the country doing the clubs. Bob Block wrote most of it and, when I ventured to write a little piece, he was dead upset. It was rubbish really. We weren't used to learning scripts and someone else telling us it was funny. We were used to being instinctive and reacting to things that happened.

But there were still some amusing moments in the world of custard pies and frantically loading people up with cabbages. One dull day in the studio was brightened when Heather read the script and discovered that Syd was a toy soldier, Elaine was another toy and Heather and I were described as 'two ageing ballerinas'. She was instantly traumatised even before she went into make-up. She rushed to producer Brian Jones all flustered and said, 'How can I be an ageing ballerina? I was booked as a juvenile lead.'

He said 'Yes, dear, but it is just acting, isn't it?'

'Can't we make the ballerina younger?' she pleaded hopefully but to no avail.

I was 31 years old at the time and I was dressed in a pink tutu, a pink curly wig, tights and ballet shoes with bright-red cheeks courtesy of the make-up department. As we were just about to do this sketch, I noticed that Heather was in tears. 'What's wrong?' I asked gallantly.

'Look at me,' she sobbed. 'I'm supposed to be a juvenile lead. It's just not fair.'

My sympathy evaporated fast. I said, 'Heather, I'm the father of two, look at the state of *me*. If anybody should be crying, it's me.' I think that cheered her up a little bit.

But it was a horrendous experience really, because all of a sudden we had this split life. We'd go from dancing around doing kids' sketches to hurtling up to rough clubs in the north-east or wherever and belting out some strong stuff to keep the drunks happy.

You had to be hard-hitting to survive in the clubs and it took us ages to shake off the kiddie image. The BBC sanitised us on the television but we never looked on ourselves as children's entertainers.

Crackerjack nearly killed me for real. I had a car crash late one night following Syd back over the Pennines. Syd was only about half a mile in front of me when I came to this bend and skidded on some ice and went right through a wall. It was like *The Italian Job* because the car was balanced over a drop. Fortunately, it was dark so I couldn't see how dangerous it was. The police stopped and recognised me and gave me a lift home. I was still up early the next day and back down to London to do *Crackerjack*.

I love the world of pantomime for the whole surreal lunacy of the event. One of my favourite panto moments came when we were in Bristol from Christmas 1974 doing *Jack and the Beanstalk*.

OPPORTUNITY KNOCKS

Mark Wynter, quite a serious chap, was playing Jack. I think he thought he was Errol Flynn at times, but to be fair the panto was full of high drama. There were lots of other things as well, but there was certainly high drama. The giant sat at a big desk with a harp on it and on top of the harp was a little ventriloquist's dummy's head. It was on the end of a long stick and, whenever the giant woke up and said, 'Fee, Fi, Fo, Fum', the young lad who was operating the dummy's head used to lift him up about an inch as if he was frightened of this huge scary giant. It was Dora Bryan's son who used to do it but, when he had to go back to university, they needed someone else to do it.

Step forward Dave the roadie. Syd's brother was over the moon to be asked to take over the job. But Dave doesn't do things by halves. He decided to give the dummy a complete makeover. Next minute the dummy's head, on its big long stick, was in our dressing room and Dave was sandpapering it, making it up, combing its long Beatles-style hair, and really tidying it up.

Next day at the matinee, when the moment came for the giant to wake up, he started his speech with, 'Fee...', and the dummy's head shot up about five feet in the air, and on the way down it shook so its hair was all over the place. 'Fo...' Up again. And so it went on. Well, all the stage hands and everyone in the panto knew that Dave was doing it and they all started to laugh. The audience didn't know any different and they laughed at the exaggerated movements as well. Everyone was in stitches. Normally, the dummy's head hardly moved but now it was going up and down and round and round and everyone was laughing fit to burst. The usherettes were laughing in the aisles, and Dora Bryan was in absolute hysterics.

At the end of the show, everyone was slapping Dave on the back, telling him how funny it was. But he didn't look very happy. I asked him what was wrong. 'I've just been sacked,' he said grimly.

Evidently, Mark Wynter thought it was a very serious scene and Dave was taking the limelight away from him. He only lasted for one performance and then his big chance was gone. Everybody was outraged, when they stopped laughing.

One of the best panto producers was Humphrey Stanbury. He always tried to do something different, particularly one show at Wolverhampton. It was *Robinson Crusoe* and, in one scene, Man Friday is tied to the stake in the jungle, so Humphrey thought it would be good to have some lions on the stage. They were to be in cages, obviously, but he was still determined to try to make it look as if they were going to eat Man Friday. He made some arrangements with the local zoo but, when the curtains opened for this chilling scene, the audience was treated to the not too frightening sight of these lions fast asleep! Humphrey was not happy.

The owner apologised but explained that they were

two male lions that knew each other so they were never going to look too lively. He suggested he brought a male and a female lion for the next performance, which was more likely to produce some snarling. It was the Boxing Day matinee and the theatre was packed. The curtains opened to reveal two lions doing what comes naturally to all animals, very energetically. It was quite a shock. There was a moment of deathly silence in the theatre until they panicked and shut the curtains. Humphrey was not happy.

In the spring of 1976, we did a short tour with Gene Pitney. We had toured with him back in 1965 and he said he was surprised to see how far we had progressed in the 11 years since then. The tour took us back to my home city of Glasgow, where I received a visit from the stage-door keeper who wanted to know if my real name was McGinnis. I told him it was and wondered why he wanted to know. He said my uncle Hughie was at the stage door asking for me. Naturally, I rushed down to meet him.

Hughie was my dad's eldest brother and he was with his wife, my auntie Annie, and my auntie Frankie (who was my dad's youngest sister). I was really chuffed to see them all because I hadn't set eyes on them since I left Glasgow as a boy in 1952.

'How's yer father?' asked my auntie Frankie.

'He's OK,' I replied.

'Yer faither was the best-looking of all the McGinnises,' she remarked proudly.

'He isn't now,' I said. 'He is bigger than me.'

She was annoyed and said, 'Don't you talk about yer faither like that, yer faither has got lovely teeth.'

I replied, 'He keeps them by the side of the bed right now.'

She said, 'Don't you talk about my brother like that,' and slapped me smartly across the face. 'See you, Teddy McGinnis. If you're nae good tonight, I'm going to come up on stage and show you up.' She didn't make an appearance, thank goodness, so I must have been all right.

The Major was instrumental in getting us on to a new TV show called *Who Do You Do?* but, because he didn't know anything about the ethics of the business, he was becoming a liability. In the days when Bernard Delfont was the king of showbusiness, the Major would walk into Delfont's London headquarters and say, 'Excuse me, Bernie, I was just passing,' which could be an effective tactic but could also get up some very important noses.

The Major also managed Paper Lace when they had their number-one hit. He was starting to get distracted by the pop business just at the time we needed someone to guide us.

We made a switch to London Management and found a very impressive young man called Michael Grade was our new agent. He was a breath of fresh air, a very clever man indeed. I always feel sorry for Michael that certain newspapers remember him more for the pornography on Channel 4 than for creating the slots for *EastEnders* that helped to rescue the ratings for BBC. However, I suppose the chairman of the BBC hardly needs my sympathy.

After Michael got involved, doors started to open. We got on the Palladium with Cliff Richard for a six-week season. Being on *Sunday Night at the London Palladium* was a fantastic thrill. Michael's father booked the acts there. We started to move forward. When Michael moved to London Weekend Television, a guy called Norman Murray inherited us, and it was a case of him splitting us off from the Major. In June 1975, we split, although he still collected 15 per cent of our earnings right up to 1977, which went up a lot during those years. He did all right out of it.

Norman Murray was from the old school of showbusiness, very much a theatre man. He was a brilliant negotiator but very hard. He knew everybody and he had been in the job since he was 15 but that was his weakness in a way. He could put together great bills for the old theatrical shows, but those days had long gone. There were no places even then for the jugglers and the plate-spinners.

The power was shifting. The clubs were now king of the live scene and the heyday of the theatres was over. Acts like ours could earn a lot of money without any need for a big variety bill and I don't think many people really knew how to deal with that. Norman was a fearsome agent to have on your side. I overheard him once say that, if your act buys a Mercedes, then next time get him to buy a Ferrari and he will always need you.

We were once in one of Norman Murray's pantos, in Bradford, and typically when it came to budgeting he was determined to leave no corner uncut. We had a ghost scene but we didn't have anyone to play the ghost. 'Oh, the company manager will do it,' said Norman airily.

The company manager was of a nervous disposition and pretty alarmed at the prospect of playing a ghost. There was no costume so we decided he would just have to put a sheet over his head. We rehearsed without the sheet, and he seemed to get the hang of it, but, on the first performance, he came on, did his scaring act from underneath the sheet and then fell headlong into the orchestra pit. Fortunately, he landed on the drums so he didn't do himself any serious damage but he still just about brought the house down. It turned out that he hadn't put any eyeholes in the sheet.

We were appearing in Gloucester when we were invited to audition for what turned out to be a new impressionists' comedy show called *Who Do You Do?*. We had to go to Fulham where we met a highly intimidating producer called Jon Scoffield. He was a good-looking guy who strutted around like a male model and, if he had a sense of humour at all, he kept it a closely guarded secret. It looked as if it would be easier to make a statue laugh but we did some little bits out of our act and we were in.

Our version of Laurel and Hardy evidently appealed to the enigmatic Mr Scoffield. Daley and Wayne were on the show as well, and we were upset to be accused of copying them. We didn't, of course, as I'd never seen them until much later. When I did see Bill and Paddy at work, I could see what people meant, but they were a speciality act and there was no way we could have copied their routines even if we'd tried.

Freddie Starr was on the show along with Roger Kitter, Paul Melba and others. Scoffield seemed to like us because he decreed we could do double stuff. I used to do Harry Secombe and Syd did Eccles, which was great. We just did our act and Scoffield sliced it up into 15-second segments in front of a white backdrop and made it look very fast and furious. It was quite groundbreaking in its day.

Jon Scoffield was one of television's great characters but he also had a reputation in the business for frostiness. They called him the 'chest freezer' at one TV company because of the cold front he presented. I never did get to understand him, although he also produced one of our pantomimes. On the other hand, he said to me one day, 'I don't understand you. When you're with your friend, you're OK but, when you're on your own, no.'

'That's because we're a double act,' I said.

'Hmm,' he said, 'very strange.'

He always used to have a pop at us. He could be very grumpy when he put his mind to it. There is a famous story about the time Scoffield was head of entertainment at ATV and phoned up a well-known Birmingham comic called Dave Ismay to ask him about hosting *Bullseye*, a brand-new quiz show. Not wanting to appear too keen, Dave said, 'I'll just have a look in my diary.' Scoffield told him not to bother and then phoned Jim Bowen. Jim was quick to accept the job, which subsequently made him a figure of some national hilarity and a millionaire. According to the story, every year Jim sends Dave a diary.

Jon used to wear some amazing outfits. I recall an actor from a period play walking into the Thames canteen dressed in huge boots, a cloak and an enormous medallion on a massive chain. Someone brought the house down when he said, 'I think Jon has gone over the top this time.' I just wish it had been me. Jon worked very successfully with Freddie Starr but it was never an easy relationship. Freddie used to become frustrated and walk out of the studio when it all got too much.

The trouble with work is that too often it gets in the way of the really important things in life like football in general and Manchester City in particular. While we were in *Jack and the Beanstalk* in Wolverhampton in 1976, City made it through to the League Cup Final. I couldn't get away because we had a matinee and I have to confess I did a very unprofessional thing. I went on stage with a little radio in my pocket with the earpiece in my ear. Fortunately, long hair was fashionable in those days so I was able to hide it.

The script had Syd saying, 'You're frightened of the giant, aren't you?' and me replying, 'No, I am not. If I meet him, I'll smash him in the kneecaps,' and then the giant would loom up behind me and the kids would go mad. But just as Syd was doing his line I heard in my ear that Peter Barnes had scored for City and my answer came out as: 'Yes. Yes. Yes.' Syd, the giant and the audience were all very confused for a moment or two.

After winning *Opportunity Knocks*, I thought Thames TV, who made the long-running talent show, might have thought we had some screen potential. But evidently the studio bosses were broadly underwhelmed by our appeal.

Just one man had faith. Roy Mayoh knew we had it in us to do well on television and he kept plugging away with ideas for us. Eventually, one stuck and *The Little and Large Tellyshow* was first seen in a pilot just before Christmas 1976. It was well received and a series was swiftly commissioned which was screened the following spring. By then we were really on a roll.

We had an amazing year in 1977. Our first TV series went on the air and we did the *Royal Variety Show* with Tommy Cooper, which the Americans took over and retitled *America Salutes the Queen*, because it was the Jubilee year. But the American producers couldn't understand Tommy. He turned up and asked, 'When do you want me?' in that unmistakable voice. They looked baffled but they said it was a 12 o'clock start.

At noon the next day, there was no sign of Tommy so they just had to rehearse everything else. At midnight, Tommy walked in. The Americans were screaming but Tommy just said, 'You said to be here at 12 o'clock.'

The stagehands were falling about laughing but the Americans definitely did not get the joke.

We've got a full set, they said. I don't want that, said Tommy, I've got my curtain, my gap and my table. The Americans gave up. The only musician left was the rehearsal pianist an dTommy was asking if it would be louder on the night. The Americans were screaming that they had a 32-piece orchestra. It'll be louder. I'm going to go over here and do trick, trick, trick, just follow me. The English producer got a word in and said, 'Oh, just leave him, it'll be all right on the night', and of course it was. It was more than all right and Tommy was brilliant as usual.

It didn't start off so brilliantly for us, though. Bob Hope introduced us as Little and George in the rehearsal which made us both feel pretty small. Syd was mortified and, of course, he wanted me to tell the great man instantly that he'd got our name wrong. Mercifully, he got it right on the night. Bob was reading everything off cards and our names were written up even bigger just so Bob didn't make the same mistake again.

When we did the dress rehearsal, we were double nervous so we had Dave with us that night. He used to protect our props with his life and shout, 'Mind my props,' at anyone who wandered too near to our humble gear. But at the dress rehearsal there was a panic. We were coming down the big steps for our entrance and the table wasn't there. Our opening song 'Do You Wanna Touch...' was blasting out and it wasn't ready. So it was a bit of a shambles as a run through. I was devastated. This was so important to us and of all things our props were missing.

We got through it somehow but that night I found out what it was to have a completely sleepless night. I didn't get a wink. As a big treat I was in the Waldorf Hotel with Sandra and the kids. The American impressionist Rich Little was on the show as well, so I had to be careful what impressions I did.

We were like nervous wrecks. After the performance, we were so relieved, and we went in to meet some of the other acts. Rich Little was in there with Paul Anka and they were dissecting Tommy Cooper's act, and they just didn't have a clue. Tommy did these wonderfully simple things like throwing a bunch of flowers over his shoulder and then turning round and looking shocked, 'For me?' It made me laugh and it still does, but Rich Little and Paul Anka analysed it so deeply they talked the humour out of it. In spite of the fact that Tommy had gone down a storm, they were sneering and very critical. I felt like storming in and saying, '**** off, this is Tommy.' But for once I restrained myself. I don't believe in analysing comedy too deeply.

Tommy's wife Dove tells my favourite story about him. She tells it very sadly, but to me it is simply funny. Mind you, I wasn't married to him.

Tommy comes home from the pub at one o'clock in the morning and he brings a mate back to the house with him. Dove is furious that he's back so late and comes flying down the stairs. She's had a few herself and she's got her mudpack on. 'What ****ing time do you call this? The pub closed hours ago. Where have you been?' And she really lays into Tommy and his pal.

Next day, when they wake up, Tommy says, 'That was terrible what you did last night. You didn't know who that fellow was. You could have cost me a film. He could have been a Hollywood producer. You could have ruined my career.' He really made her feel awful and she promised that she would never do anything like that again.

A few nights later and it's one o'clock in the morning and Dove is alone in the house again. She hears the door go and she hears Tommy's voice say, 'Come in, Charlie, what are you having to drink?'

'What are you having, Tommy?'

'I'm going to have a G and T,' says Tommy.

'I'll have the same, Tom.'

Dove sits upstairs listening to them, and they have more drinks and more drinks and slowly but surely as they carried on the two voices became one. Dove creeps down the stairs and Tommy's sitting on the settee on his own doing the two voices. Dove told me the story to illustrate what a terrible state Tommy's drinking had got to. I can see that but it just makes me laugh so much.

Tommy was a one-off. He is supposedly the first person to hand over a teabag and say, 'Get yourself a drink.' Tommy was a natural. He was just a genuinely funny man. But it's not always easy being a comic. If you go into a pub, you feel you have to give a performance because people obviously expect you to be funny.

CHAPTER SIX

Patsy

I was married to Sandra for 13 years before I even met Patsy, although the marriage had sadly long since run out of steam. It was nobody's fault, really, but I was concentrating on my career, which was going well, and Sandra never wanted to be a part of that. She didn't like the limelight and she found many of the people in the business brash and phoney. Perhaps she has a point there, but Syd and I had worked very hard to scramble up those bottom rungs of the showbiz ladder. And, now we were on our way up, we were determined to enjoy our moment of fame, whether it was to last for 15 minutes or 15 years.

I met Patsy for the first time in Liverpool. We had just done *The Little and Large Tellyshow* so we were catapulted into the limelight. We went on to do a summer season in Blackpool, which was phenomenal thanks to our sudden screen success, and we had old friends Frank Carson, Jim Davidson and Norman Collier to make sure we never stopped laughing. I later had peritonitis and had to have six weeks off, after which we went on to do pantomime in Liverpool with Norman Collier, Charlie Caroli and a really good cast, including Maria Morgan who was the Princess and one Patsy Ann Scott who was playing Aladdin. There was even a very young Tracey Ullman in the line-up. She was a cheeky girl but, of course, at the time we had no idea she would go so far.

I suppose I was vaguely aware of Patsy before then because she was already appearing on the popular ITV quiz show *3-2-1*. At the time, she was just another member of the company, very pretty and very professional, and the thought honestly never crossed my mind that we might one day get together. I was going home nearly every night. There was no romance that year.

We did all become friends but Patsy went off from our panto to do another show at Bristol that was running longer than our show. One of Patsy's lines in *Aladdin* was 'What is it?' and it became a sort of in-joke between us, so we sent her a good luck telegram as she opened in Bristol saying 'What is it?' from Syd and Eddie. *Aladdin* was just a very happy company: any company with Norman Collier in is full of laughs. No one is allowed to be miserable when Collier is in the vicinity.

PATSY

When we were lower down the bill, we often thought people at the top didn't treat us quite right, so we always vowed that if we ever got up there we would do it better. And we did. We used to give a bottle of champagne to all the principals and we'd give out chocolates and beer to other people. We gave out birthday presents as well, and Tracey Ullman's birthday was in January: I remember giving her a box of chocolates. I think she thought there was an ulterior motive but there wasn't. Unfortunately, we got done by the Inland Revenue for claiming the money back. We said paying for drinks and a last-night party was goodwill but they said it wasn't tax deductible and we had to pay all the money back.

The following year we were with quite a lot of the same company in panto in Oxford, which was when Patsy and I got together, although we were friends for a long time before we were lovers. We all used to go in a big gang to a fabulous Chinese restaurant to wind down after the show. The gang usually included Syd and his wife, Norman Collier and his wife, and Maria Morgan.

I liked Patsy as a person because she was so warm and bubbly but it took a long time for the attraction between us to grow. It was winter and we were all working hard together and you do become close. You never go out on your own and I was pretty well past the disco stage by this time. Our relationship was very innocent for a long time but maybe I'm a bit slow on the uptake. Patsy even came Christmas shopping with me around the streets of Oxford to help me buy presents for Sandra and the girls.

Very slowly, the friendship turned into something more. We started to find ourselves on our own after everyone else had drifted off home. I think it came as a surprise to both of us. Patsy's dad George used to come and fetch her home on Sunday and I got to know him slowly as well. It was a genuine friendship that grew into love. It sounds corny but it wasn't. There was a big gap in that side of my life by then. It wasn't anyone's fault that Sandra and I just grew apart. I tried to be there for my daughters but it was difficult for everyone.

One night, we came out of the restaurant late with Maria, who was about six months pregnant by then. I took Patsy and Maria back to the pub where they were staying and we found it was all in darkness and locked up. We banged on the door but we couldn't make anyone hear. I said, 'You'll have to come back to stay the night with me.' I was lodging in a flat above a pub out near Thame. The girls slept in the bed and I slept on the sofa, gentleman that I am.

In the morning, the landlady, who was a bit fearsome, was quite shocked when I walked down followed by two very attractive young women, especially as one of them was six months pregnant. I said, 'Now, I know this looks bad...' and I burbled out an explanation. 'This is the Princess – she's pregnant – and this is Aladdin.' I think the landlady saw the funny side of it eventually.

As the weather got bad, I decided to move into

Top left: Me as a baby.

Top right: My cousin had a wedding in Glasgow 1949 when I was seven. I'm second from the left. My sister is far left on the bottom row, she's two-and-a-half.

Middle right: I was 15 in this school picture, standing at the back on the left.

Bottom: A school play – I'm on the left.

Top: Me in the middle of my mates on a lads' night out. Later in the evening we got barred from the pub for 'high spirits'.

Middle: Another trip for the lads, this one to Blackpool in 1962. I'm on the floor at the front wearing sunglasses and Syd is to my right. I wanted to use this photo because if everyone in it buys a book, that's 22 copies.

Right: Norbrook Boys Club. I'm in the middle wearing the Puma boots I bought with money lent to me by Mr Shatwell (standing far left).

Top: Syd singing 'Speedy Gonzales' while I do the lalala-ing.

Middle left: Performing at the Yew Tree Hotel in 1963.

Middle right: Little and Large – 1964 model.

Right: An early publicity postcard.

Top: The Royal Variety Show in 1977. Meeting the Queen with, on my right, Muppets men Jim Henson and Frank Oz – a proud moment.

Middle: Doing the act in Hastings.

Bottom: Ryan makes his stage debut, aged 20 months.

Top left: Guernsey in the summer of 1971. Clockwise from top left, Sammy, Paul, Alison and Donna. Sammy and Alison are my kids, the other two are Syd's.

Top right: My dad, Teddy, snatching the mic off Lulu.

Middle right: Dave the roadie gets in on the act.

Bottom: At my wedding with the best man, my brother Brian.

Top: More from my wedding.
There's me, Teddy my dad, Jessie
my mum, Patsy, her mum Dolly
and her dad George.

Middle: We're behind him!
Panto in 1986 with Frank Bruno.

Bottom: Bobby Moore and his
wife Stephanie, Kevin Keegan
and his wife Jean and me and
Patsy in a Marbella restaurant.
Two England captains and one
failed footballer.

Top left: Golf with Seve.

Top right: Eddie Large Golf Day – Bruce, me and Jethro.

Middle: The Eddie Large Golf Classic at the Bristol and Clifton Golf Club. I'm with Jimmy Tarbuck and Ronnie Corbett.

Bottom: My long-awaited *Pro-Celebrity Golf* debut with Mike Reid, me, Gary Player, Arnold Palmer and Peter Allis.

Top: My daughter Samantha's wedding to Peter in September 1991. From the left are George and Dolly (the in-laws), Ryan – aged eight – and me and Patsy on the right.

Middle: The big red book: the moment when Michael Aspel sprung *This Is Your Life* on us in 1993.

Bottom: From left to right – Ryan, Patsy, me, my daughter Alison and her partner Chris and Samantha and Peter.

Oxford and I stayed at the Randolph Hotel, which was where Patsy and I eventually did get to know each other rather better.

The Randolph Hotel has a special place in my heart but it gave me a laugh one night as well. I got back late one night after going to the Chinese restaurant. The night porter said to me very confidentially, 'There's a mate of yours in here tonight.' I asked who it was but he thought it was a bit of a laugh not to tell me. 'I'm not telling you,' he said with a grin. 'But he is in the room facing yours, one of your best mates.'

I was intrigued and when I got to the room I noticed the room occupant he was talking about had left a menu out for breakfast. I took a sneaky look to read the signature, Sir Alec Guinness. That raised a laugh. Sir Alec was a wonderful actor but we never met. Some people have a very strange idea that everyone at any level of the entertainment business is one big happy family. I'd hate to disillusion people like the night porter but it's not quite like that.

Patsy and I didn't really expect anything to come of it because, after the panto, I went away for two weeks' holiday and Patsy went off to Portugal for a month. An awful lot of panto love affairs end with the final curtain of the last night and I was terrified that would happen to us. I knew I loved her by then and I thought she felt the same way but I was not confident. I had never met anyone quite like Patsy; I definitely didn't want to lose her. The holidays were a huge test for us and, in the back of my mind, I feared that it wouldn't last. Patsy had a boyfriend in the background as well but we knew then that we wanted to be together.

I spent a fortune telephoning Portugal and trying to get through to Patsy to make sure she hadn't forgotten all about me. But, when Patsy came back, the feeling was very strong between us. It wasn't easy. I had my children to consider and I desperately didn't want to upset them. It was an awful lot for Patsy to take on.

So getting together was not a decision taken lightly. There was an awful lot of heart-searching and agonising before we took the plunge because there were other people involved. I was no longer living at home by then but I was still married. My main concern was for my two daughters who were still only young. Obviously, it was painful for them and I still deeply regret hurting them. Happily, we have been able to rebuild those relationships and we are close again.

Nearly everyone in the business goes the same way. They meet someone in pantomime, get tempted and their marriage breaks up. It's sad in a way, but almost inevitable.

I have this theory about what happens during panto, with everyone thrust together in this mythical village. I never went with anyone while we were on a summer season, for instance, because I was always golfing. But in panto you find yourself calling each other by their panto names, 'Hello, Baron', and all that, and get caught up in a crazy world where lots of romances start. When you get back to real life, it is frequently very difficult to adjust, and often the relationship doesn't last, but I am very pleased to say that mine and Patsy's did. Actors have a saying: 'It doesn't count on location.' I really miss the friendship and the camaraderie of the filming. Everyone is away from home and you're all in it together. It can be very intoxicating.

The news of our relationship did not break straight away so we were able to have a wonderful honeymoon period together before we started hitting the headlines. I had split up from Sandra and told her what was going on. Obviously, it was very upsetting for her. I was working in Blackpool and driving across the country twice a week to see Patsy who was by then working with Freddie Starr in Scarborough.

One day, someone tipped off the press and a reporter called saying he knew we were together. I didn't really say much, just 'Yes' and 'No', but for a journalist that's enough. The coverage shocked us. We were all over the papers. My solicitor said he didn't know I was that famous and I think it was meant to be a compliment! It was a horrendous ordeal for us because we knew the cruel and intrusive publicity was hurting our families.

And we had to go on with our jobs. It's hard entertaining people when all you can think about is that they've just read about your private life in the papers. There were some very traumatic moments. I remember in Blackpool I was still taking a difficult and emotional phone call from my family when I could hear our introduction music playing. Norman Collier was frantically helping me put my jacket on, and I was crying my eyes out just before I ran on stage to try to pretend I was the funniest person in the world. It was not easy, but it's then you find out who your friends are, and my mates were very good. Syd was very supportive as well. He knew exactly what I was going through as he had done the same thing.

Freddie Starr claimed he had known all along that we were together but he hadn't wanted to say anything. There is a very kind side to Freddie that he tries to keep hidden away. I'll never forget that he wrote to me and advised me not to hide Patsy away when she came to see me. Or, as he elegantly put it, 'Walk down the promenade in Blackpool hand-in-hand with your dick out, singing zippity-doodah!' He's not exactly Claire Rayner, Freddie.

In September 1979, I split from Sandra. What a year that was. We broke up and I went to live in Blackpool on my own, and then Patsy and I got together after the summer season finished. Patsy had a little place in Notting Hill Gate in London and from there we went to live in Gerrards Cross the next year. The publicity dragged on, and each time I knew it was hurting Sandra and my daughters and I still regret that. It was a dreadful time. I've always tried to be straight about newspapers and publicity but it was horrible being followed about and photographed. Even months later, when we went on holiday, we were stopped at the airport and they rang Sandra to ask her what she thought of us flying off somewhere.

We were sitting targets for the press. For them, it was a brilliant story. Heartless comedian abandons his wife and the mother of his two children for a younger woman. In fact, Patsy was older than Sandra, but never let the facts get in the way of a good story. We were being followed around and photographed and I didn't object. I couldn't object. It was true that Patsy and I had fallen in love. We didn't want to conduct our private life in the pages of the tabloids, but I'm a grown-up. I know that in our business that sort of attention goes with the territory. My ex-wife Sandra was having a pop at Patsy and at me in the papers and I knew I just had to grin and bear it and hope everyone concerned could come through this difficult time as unscathed by the experience as possible. I have never answered back my wife's criticism to this day and I think my daughters appreciate that.

At the time, Lennie Bennett was with Max Clifford and doing a lot of publicity, including a *News of the World* double-page spread about how he and his wife Margaret were inseparable. They were so close that he wouldn't do a show if she wasn't sitting in the audience. They even shared baths together so they could soak in the same oils and share the same fragrance. Then Lennie announced in the article that he couldn't do what Eddie Large had done and abandon his loving wife and the mother of his children for another woman. He had a real go at me, saying I had heartlessly walked out on my wife to be with this 'sex machine'.

I don't get the *News of the World* so I didn't know anything about this at first. Then the phone calls started. I do have a temper and I started to get really angry. I was staying in Sheffield and I got a paper and then I really did erupt. If anyone else had said it, or someone I didn't know, then I don't think it would have bothered me so much, but it was Lennie. I'm still with Patsy after more than 25 years. He is not with Margaret any more. The proof is there and for him to criticise me I thought was beyond the pale.

I was determined to have a go at him. I rang all over the place and finally tracked him down staying at the home of an agent called Alan Field. He came on the phone all brazen and said, 'I know what you're going to say. I know what you're going to say. It was the reporter. He said his tape was off and it was just an afterthought when he asked me about you. I didn't mean to say it like that.'

But I just let rip at him. He was doing the *Lennie and Jerry* show on BBC at the same time we were doing our series and we met later in the BBC foyer. He wanted to come out with an apology. I assume. But I wasn't interested in his apologies. I just cut him off and gave him an earful of abuse, studded, I'm afraid, with as many swear words as I could remember at the time. It did lose part of its impact as I kept getting interrupted by kids asking for my autograph, so I had to keep turning away from Lennie and trying to be polite for a moment or two, before turning back to continue having a go at Lennie. Syd was as annoyed as me. We had this big public argument and, of course, the next week in the *News of the World* it said, 'Eddie Large has a verbal punch-up with Lennie Bennett. Eddie led with a left by saying blah, blah, blah then Lennie countered with a right by saying blah, blah, blah and Eddie hit Lennie with a knockout blow by saying blah, blah, blah.'

Our Dave, Syd's brother, read all this at home and he was astonished. 'Ed,' he shouted down the phone at me. 'You ****ing beat him up. Brilliant.'

I said, 'No, Dave...'

'It's here in the *News of the World*. You knocked him out.'

'No, Dave, it was just a verbal punch-up.' It took some explaining and I had to see the funny side even though I was still really annoyed by Lennie's comments. I've seen him a few times since and, as the years go on, you just have to learn to laugh with these things. But it upset me at the time because that was a fellow professional having a go, and one who should definitely have known better. I was getting stick from everywhere at the time and it was not a very nice time in my life.

I accepted all the blame for our break-up because I *was* to blame. I am not making excuses. Syd would make a brilliant excuse and everyone would feel sorry for him because he is a master at generating sympathy.

He's a genius. If he went into prison for armed robbery captured live on television, within 20 minutes he would have them all demonstrating to let him out because it wasn't really his fault. I'm more realistic. We had an injunction in our divorce to say that we would not talk about each other in the press. Sandra wanted it. So I agreed but I wanted to get it all over with. For years afterwards, just as we were starting a new series or appearing somewhere, there would be a picture of Sandra and the girls looking sad and it would all be dragged up again.

One of those times was when Patsy and I got married, four years after Sandra and I separated. We were married on 5 June 1983 and, even that day, I had a reporter following me down the aisle asking me what I thought my ex-wife felt about the ceremony. She apologised afterwards, said she was frightened of losing her job and just following orders. Otherwise, it was a wonderful day. Michael Barrymore was there and Norman Collier, Jess Conrad and loads of our friends. By then, our son Ryan had been born and we were really starting to feel like a family.

I could have tried to hit Sandra with the injunction of silence that she had insisted on, and ultimately you can get sent to prison if you break the terms of an injunction. But I just wanted it all to be over and I didn't want to upset Sandra or my daughters.

Recently, my granddaughter Holly was one and I asked my daughter Sam if she was having a party. 'Yes,' she said, 'I'm going to have some people round to the house.' I said I'd be there, but she said Sandra wouldn't come if I was there. I couldn't believe it. It was all those years ago and she won't be in the same house with me. And Sam was embarrassed to tell me. My daughters are great with me now. One is 34 and the other is 38, grown women. Sandra has never remarried.

I felt sorry for Patsy through all of this and I tried to protect her but often I simply wasn't able to. She says it was my humour that first attracted her and we both needed a sense of humour to get through those early years.

Of course, life goes on and pantomime always brings its own peculiar problems that sometimes make you wonder if life might have been easier if you'd stayed on working in the factory. At the panto in Oxford, we had a new agent called Norman Murray. He was a hard bastard who was always trying to cut corners and save money.

We had enjoyed great success with *Aladdin* in Liverpool, but, when we arrived with what we thought was the same show in Oxford, there was no director. We turned to Norman who said, 'Well, you did it all right last year, surely you can just do it again.'

'No, Norman,' we explained, 'it doesn't work like that. We've got to have a director.'

There was a row and it was decided the lad who played the villain, John Gower, would direct us.

We were nearly all the same cast, except the genie in Liverpool, a black guy called Joseph who was really good, had asked for more money. Norman Murray refused to pay it and got another black lad who he had just picked out of the actors showcase book *Spotlight*. The new guy, Bert Francis, was a big strong good-looking lad who was a bit like a young Mohammad Ali. He was a boy dancer who got another fiver for playing the genie as well.

We were doing the read-through and I was sitting next to Norman Collier who laughs at anything. You could tell Bert was a bit nervous. Flash, the trapdoor came up, cue genie: 'Command and obey, oh master,' said Bert in the campest voice you've ever heard. Norman was on the floor wetting himself with laughter. It sounds unkind but it was very funny. That's how Bert talked; he was 'precious', as we used to say in those politically incorrect days.

Bert was desperately embarrassed, but we thought that Norman Murray had auditioned him – although of course he hadn't, he had just picked him out of a book. Bert was terribly nervous and, on the night we opened, he was still carrying the script around with him everywhere. He had it at the bottom of the trapdoor and, when Aladdin rubbed the lamp, he threw the script away. The cue came, the trapdoor opened, Bert popped up and said in the most macho voice he could manage, 'Command and obey, oh master.' It still sounded pretty camp but there was not that much laughter because they thought, if that's how he's going to play it, then that's how he's going to play it.

At the interval, Norman Murray called everyone in and yelled, 'Why didn't you tell me, Dolly?' He called everyone Dolly. 'Why didn't you tell me?'

'Tell you what, Norman?'

'About the bloody genie?'

'Thought you'd auditioned him, Norman.'

'No, I didn't audition him,' he yelled. 'I just thought he looked the part. Anyway I've come up with an idea. Two thousand years ago, he was tragically struck dumb.'

I said, 'No, you can't have a genie who can't speak. And we've got to know him now and he's a nice lad. It would destroy him if you take all his lines away. We're going to live with it.' And he got better.

Our time with Norman is full of painful memories. One of our most excruciating experiences came at the Alex in Birmingham with Jack Douglas directing. We don't battle with anyone and we never have aggro. We always like a happy ship, but we had nightmares with Jack. There was a young girl called Jane something playing Cinderella, only young but a lovely little kid. I think she'd made a record or something and they were really trying to push her. But the panto was just not working.

Suddenly, I said to Jack, 'We're not in this.'

'What do you mean you're not in this?'

I tried to explain. It was all a complete mess. Jack and I simply could not work together, so I did something I would never normally do – I phoned the ultimate weapon, Norman Murray.

I said, 'Norman, for the first time in our career, we are going to have to call the cavalry in. We just can't get anywhere with Jack. The show is a total mess. It's just not happening. We're not happy at all.'

'Leave it with me, Dolly. Leave it with me,' he boomed down the phone.

Also on the bill were Jill Gascoigne and Adrienne Posta, two very tough ladies, as Dandini and Prince Charming. They had both been round the block a few times, acting-wise.

Norman arrived for a dress rehearsal and said to me, 'I'm going to sit in the stalls, Dolly, and I'll make a few notes. After the show we will all sit down together and we will talk quietly about the situation and discuss it constructively and sort all the problems out.' There was no audience there, just Jack standing in the audience puffing on his pipe and watching when he was not required on stage as Baron Hardup.

We'd just done one of our little spots and were in our dressing room when we heard this noise coming out of the Tannoy system. Dave our roadie came flying in and said, '****ing Norman Murray is doing his nut out there.'

We went out and we could hear Norman yelling through the loudspeaker system, 'Get the cow near the mike. Get the cow near the mike.'

We looked on stage and poor Jane was right at the

back singing 'When I Need Love' very softly and she was not miked up.

'Get the cow near the mike,' screamed Norman over and over again.

Jack was horrified, as though a lunatic had been let into the building. 'Get out of my theatre,' he shouted.

He and Norman had a real shouting match, with Norman, who would never back down to anybody, yelling, 'You'll never work again.'

Jill was about to come on with Adrienne and they thought it was some sort of mad protesters or something. We were thinking, Oh no, what has Norman gone and done now?

Next thing we knew, Jill kicked the door open and yelled at me and Syd, 'Is that your ****ing agent out there?'

'Er, yes, it is,' we admitted with a joint wince.

'He's a ****ing madman,' she screamed, and it was hard to disagree.

It was chaos for a while. Jack screamed at us, 'What's your agent doing interrupting my rehearsal?' That's what Norman was like – very hard. He was a very good agent. He was the agent for Michael Barrymore and Les Dawson, so he could obviously handle himself. He was a very hard man, a good negotiator. He used to say there are only two ways of doing things: 'My way and my way.' Gradually, it was sorted out but, of course, that put the lid on that panto. They all hated us after that.

It was the worst panto I've ever been involved with. Everything went wrong. It was the first panto we had done without any of our cohorts from the office. Normally, we had pals like Norman Collier, Pepe's Puppets and a marvellous actor called Peter Lewis who always played the villain, and it became like a little Rep company. With hindsight, to suddenly go in with strangers was a mistake.

We were doing *Cinderella*, but how could we do *Cinderella* if I was going to be Buttons? What was Syd going to be? So we suggested Bows. Buttons and Bows, the two servants, because we never liked being conventional. If it was *Aladdin*, they said we could be Wishy and Washee, but we didn't want to do that so we became Aladdin's brothers and it worked very well. In *Jack and the Beanstalk*, it worked well with us being the new characters of Jack's brothers. But, in *Cinderella*, Buttons and Bows somehow just didn't work.

There was the apple scene, when Cinderella is 16. We came to the rehearsal, and Jack was booming out his instructions. I gave her the apple as Buttons and Jane in her strong Welsh accent said, 'Ooh, I like apples. Do you like apples, Buttons?'

We rehearsed the whole scene and it was all a bit tense. Then Jane came out of character and said, 'Does it have to be an apple?'

'Well, yes,' said Jack. 'It's the tradition.'

'I don't like apples,' said Jane. 'Could we use something else?'

'What?' said Jack, completely nonplussed by this sudden tangent.

'What about a banana?' said Jane. 'I like bananas.'

The whole company collapsed as Jack desperately tried to explain why it really *had* to be an apple but the whole panto was like that, just a mess.

There's always a lot of hanging around, and Patsy, who was pregnant with Ryan, used to sit a lot in our dressing room knitting. Jack came in and saw what she was doing and said, 'Bad luck, bad luck. You shouldn't knit in a dressing room. It will bring doom and gloom.' Maybe he was right.

Early on, Jack confided in me, 'I'm going to teach you about the fourth wall. I'm going to make you an actor.'

I thought, how can you have a fourth wall in panto? 'Hello, boys and girls. I'm sorry I can't see or hear you. There's a ****ing big wall in the way.'

Poor old Bob Grant, who had been in *On The Buses* with Reg Varney, was in the show playing an Ugly Sister and didn't turn up for a couple of nights. He was a lovely fellow but I think he'd had enough of it as well. He did a runner.

None of these problems really bothered me, however, and the reason for that was Patsy. For the first time in my life I was totally in love and felt I had found my ideal partner. I am not that good at showing my real emotions. Like a lot of comics, too often I hide them behind a joke. But now I knew I could face any difficulty or hardship with Patsy by my side. At the risk of going all hearts and flowers I'd like to recall one of the many hilarious moments that have marked our life together.

Patsy and I were delighted when Frank Bruno became a big pal. We worked together in panto in Bristol. Patsy played Maid Marian and Frank was Robin Hood. Frank was being followed around by the ladies and gentlemen of the press for some reason or other and became a bit trapped in his hotel, always having to be escorted back and forth. So we invited him over for dinner as a bit of a release. Patsy went through the menu about 20 times, determined to cook something that Frank really liked. It was a special evening. There was Syd and Sheree, Frankie Desmond, who played the Dame, and his wife, Val, me and Patsy, and Frank.

Patsy's father George, who has sadly passed away since, said, 'Can I come to the dinner party?'

Patsy wasn't keen. 'Dad, it's going to be late, you won't be able to stay awake.'

But George was keen to meet Frank. He was a big fan, and had seen him on the telly, but he had never met a black man in his life.

Frank arrived first and plonked himself down next to George and I asked him what he wants to drink. 'I don't mind, anything, water, anything.'

'White wine?'

'OK, yeah.'

I gave him a glass but, when me and Patsy checked it in the kitchen, we realised to our horror that the wine was off. I was mortified. I rang a mate who has a bar nearby and he agreed to let me have some replacement wine. I told Frank and he said, 'Don't bother, Eddie, I'll have water.'

'No, no,' I insisted and rushed off in the car. I raced off. Patsy was desperately anxious for everything to go well. Unfortunately, she walked into our front room just in time to see George turn to Frank and say, 'It's a shame about that wine, isn't it, Frank, because our Pat, she's worked like a nigger to make everything perfect for tonight.'

Patsy almost fainted. Just then Syd and Sheree and Frankie Desmond and his wife arrived. Poor Patsy was close to hysterics and she was saying, 'You'll never believe what my dad has just said.'

Frank was brilliant, he didn't react at all. And, afterwards, when we told George what he had said he denied it adamantly. Otherwise it was a wonderful evening.

Patsy is the love of my life, but I have to confess that I have another passion... for Manchester City Football Club. In 1981, City were doing well in the FA Cup and we were playing Ipswich Town in the semi-final. Patsy and I had a holiday booked, which meant we were away in Spain on Cup Final day. I had warned her that, if City got through the Final, I would have to go. We beat Ipswich, so I had to fly back, which meant going to Malaga, then to Madrid, then to London Heathrow and home to Gerrards Cross.

It was all arranged for me to meet the team coach at

the top of Wembley Way so I could go into Wembley with the players.

Unfortunately, what happened was that the coach went flying past me with its outriders, so I had to leg it down to Wembley and get in. It was great. I think manager John Bond thought I was a sort of lucky mascot.

When we got off the bus, I turned to Roy Bailey, the team's physio and a friend of mine, and asked if I could have my ticket so I could get out of the way and go and watch the match. He said, 'You're on the bench with us.'

It was unbelievable. They even asked me to come on the pitch with the players beforehand. It was a real thrill, a very memorable day for me. I went to the festivities that night, but the next day we flew back to Madrid and then to Malaga.

I was just getting a couple of sunbeds out to continue our holiday and I saw this curly perm that looked familiar. Kevin Keegan had just done our show, so we already knew each other pretty well. He invited us to join his family on the beach and we've been friends ever since. But my love for Manchester City goes right back to boyhood. That is why it was one of my greatest thrills to be part of the party on the big day.

Brian Kidd is one of my oldest friends, but he taught me a lesson about when to keep my mouth shut. I was at a game between City and Nottingham Forest which we lost 2–1 after giving away a silly late goal. It was pretty obvious the players weren't pleased but I still managed to make matters worse in the players' lounge afterwards by saying 'Hard luck' to Brian.

'Hard luck,' he said angrily, and I thought he was going to hit me. 'It was nothing to do with hard luck, it was bloody stupid play.'

He was clearly still seething and the incident taught me there and then how passionately those in the game feel and that there are moments when it is better to keep your mouth shut.

Fast forward to a few years later, and Syd and I were working in Buxton; City were at home against Sheffield United. 'Syd,' I said. 'We'll go to the game on the way to Buxton.' Good idea.

Syd and I sat up in the stand and at half-time we were winning 2–1, so I said to Syd they're gonna love you being here as all the fans were shouting, 'Eh, Eddie, you can bring him again,' thinking Syd was some kind of lucky mascot.

Everything changed in the second half and Sheffield United stuffed us 4–2. I said to Syd, 'They're going to blame you.'

'I've not done anything,' said Syd, suddenly all defensive.

Then the comments changed: 'Don't bring him again, Eddie.' And worse, 'You're a ****ing jinx, Little.'

Syd was horrified, so I said, 'Let's go downstairs but ignore the players, they won't want to talk about it, and they certainly won't want sympathy.'

We went straight to the physio room to say goodbye

to Roy Bailey and go. Mel Machin was the manager then and he used to take every result very personally. After a bad result, he behaved as if someone had just shot his mother. And this was a *very* bad result.

Mel was leaning against the wall in the changing room and the atmosphere was not quite as happy as a funeral. All I wanted to do was catch Mel's eye and scarper. But Syd's not like that. He wants to talk to everyone he meets. So he said to the misery-stricken manager, 'Bit of hard luck that, wasn't it, Mel?'

Machin just flew at Syd. '****ing hard luck?' he screamed in Syd's face. 'Don't talk to me about ****ing hard luck! That wasn't ****ing luck! That was ****ing disgraceful!'

I bundled Syd out of the door as fast as I could and I don't think he has been to a game since.

CHAPTER SEVEN
The Bigtime

Michael Hurll is a brilliant and driven television producer. 'Hurly-Burly', as I loved to call him, played a huge part in our career and led to us switching channels to the BBC. After the first series of *The Little and Large Tellyshow* on ITV, we were halfway through a summer season in Blackpool when Michael Hurll asked us to appear on a Seaside Special.

At the time, we were not really aware of how well the Thames series had gone down with the public. During production, we were living in a pub near the studios called the Cardinal Wolsey and the shows were going out only a day or so after we recorded them. We were isolated from the reaction because we were working so hard. It was only when we got to Blackpool to start the summer season and people such as Jim Davidson and Frank Carson raced up to congratulate us that it began to sink in that we'd had a hit series. When we saw punters queuing round the block, we were on a real high.

We came from nowhere and I was really very shy about that early success. After all those years of trying, we were not remotely aware of how popular we were becoming. The power of television is immense; all of a sudden we were in danger of becoming household names, and not just in our own households! The producer kept telling us how pleased everyone was with the ratings. We were dead chuffed, but then that summer we were at the North Pier and, bingo, we were the flavour of the month.

Everyone wanted to know us. When we walked down the North Pier, everyone would stop us and want to talk. At first, I couldn't handle it. I used to try to disguise myself with hats and coats with the collar up. I even used to wear dark glasses which made not the slightest difference. My shape is not exactly easy to disguise. Fans would be shouting and I just didn't want to know. I realised I would have to try to overcome it, to develop some repartee to keep everyone happy and not have them all thinking I was just a miserable git.

So I followed Frank down the pier one day and all the little old ladies were sitting in their deckchairs. 'Hello, Mr Carson,' they'd shout. And Frank would shout back. 'Hello there. Hard luck last week in Miss

World… better luck next week in the Horse of the Year Show,' and all the punters just fell about laughing. I realised I had to have a quick comeback to give all the people who endlessly asked me, 'Where's Syd?' or whatever. I took a lesson from Frank and came up with a string of quick answers. And I still do it to this day, much to the embarrassment of my wife and family. But the public don't want to see a comedian looking miserable. My son Ryan will often say, 'Dad, we could have been home half an hour ago if you hadn't insisted on talking to everyone.'

We switched to the BBC in the summer of 1977. This came to be regarded as a fiendishly ruthless move with us determined to extract the best possible deal from the programme makers, but it wasn't quite like that. *The Little and Large Tellyshow*, made for Thames TV, was transmitted on ITV from 18 April to 30 May 1977. When all of a sudden we couldn't walk down the street without being recognised, we thought we had made it at last, yet the response from Thames afterwards was non-existent. We didn't expect tankers full of champagne or even telegrams of congratulations, but an indication of what might happen next would have been nice. We were baffled and a little let down.

That summer we agreed to appear on a *Seaside Special* with Hurly-Burly in Great Yarmouth. Hurly-Burly was very happy with the result. He came into the tent afterwards all furtive and conspiratorial and asked, 'Are you signed to Thames?'

We had to say we weren't. Nothing had been said to us about a second series.

It was also an awkward time for me because I was ill. It was the end of a funny old week at the tail of June 1977. I didn't feel very well on the Monday and, thanks to Frank Carson, we had to go to this place where they were doing a karate demonstration for charity. Frank roped us all in – me, Syd, Jim Davidson, Norman Collier and the rest of the gang. Of course, as I was supposed to be action man, they wanted to use me. I was under the weather anyway but having some karate expert waving his arms about half an inch from my nose did nothing for my state of health.

The next night we went off to another social club for another charity and I was unfortunate enough to encounter the female fan from Hell. She looked like one of those old women that Les Dawson used to dress up as. I was feeling really bad, and she came up and right in my face she shouted, 'Give us a photograph.'

'I'm sorry,' I said, 'I haven't got any photographs with me tonight.'

'Haven't got any photographs! Huh, and you're supposed to be a big star! The next time you're on the telly in our club, I'll turn it off!'

She went away and then she came back at me a bit later on. 'No photographs, eh? Can't believe it. I've had photographs from all the big stars. I got Dickie Valentine, David Whitfield, Peter Firmani.' Fair enough hitting me with Dickie Valentine and David Whitfield, I thought, they were big stars in their day, but Peter Firmani? He might be a nice fellow but I worked with him in Guernsey in 1971 and he is not a major entertainment figure. 'Sign the back of this beermat!' she yelled.

I breathed a sigh of relief but then a bit later she came back at me again. I was feeling like death warmed up and I'm afraid to say that when she turned at me and sneered, 'Call yourself a big star', I flipped and replied with a rather vulgar response delivered at maximum volume. Everyone laughed but, of course, she said, 'I always knew you were like that.' I try to be friendly and reasonable, but sometimes I don't quite manage it.

As if that wasn't bad enough, on the Friday our intrepid publicist George Bartram had arranged for me to ride a donkey on the beach because it was the anniversary of General Custer's death. I was desperate to see a doctor and eventually I got a very distracted medic who arrived in a dinner jacket. He took my temperature, which was 103. He said it was a virus, gave me something to take and said he would come back later. We went on stage and did the spot. I felt dreadful and the doctor did come back and walked round the pier with me, still insisting it was a virus.

I got home to Bury but I got worse and had to call the ambulance out. When I got to Bury General Hospital, it turned out I had acute peritonitis and was not very far from death. I'm delighted to record that the first doctor I was unfortunate enough to meet has since been struck off.

It was my birthday on the Saturday but I was in hospital. Frank Carson had organised a party and even ordered a special cake. But Frank's not one to be knowingly left out of pocket so he put an advert in the local paper: 'For Sale – Birthday Cake, would suit someone aged 36 called Eddie'. According to Frank, a man came to his house to buy the cake. He said he was 36, his name wasn't Eddie, but he wanted the cake anyway. We had to cancel and Frank stood in for us. Syd had been on a canal trip somewhere and hadn't heard what had happened. He arrived at the North Pier complaining that nobody told him anything as usual.

Sometimes the funniest humour comes from real life. I had straight hair at the time which made me look a bit different, I suppose, and as usual my life was brightened by humour. We squeezed in a lift at the hospital and this big nurse followed us in and squealed, 'Here. I know you.'

'Yeah,' I said, 'I know you do. I'm Russell Grant.'

'No, you ain't.'

'No, sorry. I'm Max Boyce.'

'No, you ain't. There be two of you. I've got it. You're Cannon and Small.'

I said, 'I'm the little one with the curly hair and moustache.'

'Ah yes,' she said. 'I've got you now.'

I went away to North Wales and stayed in a caravan to try to get over my peritonitis. I was told to phone in every day to our office but, while I was away, Norman

Murray said he was negotiating with the BBC. I was staring out at the driving rain in Abersoch while our future was decided. We were switching to the BBC, and Syd and I always felt we never had a lot of say in this decision. We were clueless, but Norman Murray made it sound as if the BBC was the place to be if you wanted to have a future in television.

We just couldn't take it all in. There wasn't a lot of enthusiasm for us from anyone in power at Thames and they were just stalling. We had become good friends with Royston Mayoh, who had given us our chance on *Opportunity Knocks* and had worked hard to get us our first series, so we wanted to stay at Thames out of loyalty to Roy. He really stuck his neck out and we enjoyed working with him very much, but a lot of the executives at Thames didn't want us at all and didn't think we were ready for a series even though the ratings told a different story. We were never fashionable and we did attract a lot of criticism, but our show went higher in the ratings than *Opportunity Knocks*, so they had to take notice of us.

The head of light entertainment was Phillip Jones, who hated Norman Collier's act. He just couldn't see anything funny in Norman at all, but we didn't know this and used him in a very funny sketch with his chicken voice. They went down well but, afterwards, in the bar, Phillip Jones came up to Norman who just said, 'I'm sorry. Who are you?' This was most unlike Norman. He must have known what the Thames head of light entertainment thought of him. But, to be fair to Phillip, he said he liked the routine but he was one of the many Thames executives who never really got behind us. I think, if they'd ever made us a proper offer, we would have stayed, but they didn't and the BBC did. In the end, we were just led by the nose by our agent. We didn't even get any more money to switch channels to the BBC.

When we left ITV, we got moaned at a lot. Hughie Green asked, 'Why didn't you take Roy with you?' but we didn't know you could do things like that.

The first show of our own we did for the BBC was *The Little and Largest Show on Earth*, recorded that autumn in a huge marquee in Belle Vue, Manchester, which had just been hit by incessant rain. We got a fabulous reaction in the tent. I thought it was going to come off its ropes. We couldn't believe it, and it took us completely by surprise. Marti Caine's long dress got very wet and Leo Sayer's white suit was pretty damp as well. Smokie sang 'Living Next Door to Alice' and the BBC had to dig a trench round the tent to get the water to run away

At the BBC, we were treated as if we were the finished article, which we weren't. The hardest thing was that we arrived there very soon after Morecambe and Wise left to join ITV. So we were tagged as the 'new Morecambe and Wise', a nightmare description for any act. No way did we want to compete with Morecambe and Wise: we loved them and knew how good they were. We were the new boys. I idolised Eric and Ernie and I still do. Eric Morecambe is one of the few people I know who can be called a comedy genius. So to be compared to them was a bit embarrassing to say the least.

The publicity didn't do us any favours at all. I had sat and watched them as a fan never dreaming that we would appear in the same places, let alone be considered a rival.

I even once went on my own as a punter to a matinee in Manchester to watch Morecambe and Wise in panto in *Sleeping Beauty* and I loved every minute of the show. Morecambe and Wise always pulled it off. I have watched them work in many theatres and ended up crying laughing. In 1964, they were on at the ABC in Blackpool. I'd had an argument with Sandra, who was my fiancee at the time, and we weren't talking, but after a few minutes of the show I was crying with laughter in spite of my personal troubles. Because of the way they made me laugh, I thought we could never rival them, but the publicity made it look that way. Inevitably, we were compared, and equally inevitably everyone said we were trying to take their place. So no pressure there then!

We just wanted to do our own thing and make people laugh. The tag of being the replacements for Morecambe and Wise hung around for a long time but we never thought it was fair or accurate.

We've had some strange experiences with the press

over the years. In our early days, we got a huge spread in the *News of the World* because the editor's daughter just happened to be a huge fan of ours. It was when we were doing our first series at Thames and we were the new kids on the block, and the editor sent their showbusiness reporter Ivan Waterman to interview us. We were staying in the Charlton Hotel, next to the Cardinal Wolsey where we used to rehearse. We met Ivan in the Chinese restaurant and did the interview over a meal.

At around 10pm, the cinema must have finished because a lot of punters came in, including a couple of young girls who recognised us and said, 'Oooh, Little and Large. How are you? Can we have your autographs?'

There was a black girl and a white girl and we signed their serviettes and turned back to continue our chat with Ivan. He winked at me and said, 'Which one is yours, Eddie? The black girl or the white one?'

I was amazed. I said, 'They've just come out of the cinema. We've never seen them before in our lives.'

He wouldn't believe that and he kept going on about it, so. at the end of the interview, we asked him to come back and have a drink in the bar so he could see for himself that the girls weren't there and there was no funny business going on. But the bar was closed and Ivan said, 'Are they upstairs, then?'

We couldn't convince him we were most certainly not seen off to dreamland by hordes of passionate groupies. Ivan was confused because the *News of the World* normally has some salacious revelation, and, for once, presumably because his daughter had suggested the idea, the editor just wanted a nice positive piece. They gave us a double-page spread that was like a free advert. I think it must have kept Ivan awake at night.

Even before we did the Thames series, we heard whispers that Thames weren't happy. People criticised us because we didn't talk to each other on stage like traditional double acts. I suppose that was us being alternative, though nobody thought that at the time. Syd and I went to a football dinner and Jimmy Tarbuck came up to us and said, 'The show is brilliant but do one series and don't do any more. Just do the one.'

We were baffled but, when I think about it, perhaps he was right. We went on to do 11 series and we became like talking wallpaper. I mean, when *Who Wants To Be A Millionaire?* came on, I used to love it and I thought I would never ever miss an edition, but now I can't be bothered. Everything has its shelf life.

We got Michael Hurll as our producer as soon as we arrived at the BBC. With the benefit of hindsight, I realise now that he wasn't really right for us. Michael is famous for his editing – we knew it was Little and Large but there was no guarantee that both of us would be in it. I remember the Grumbleweeds did a *Juke Box Jury* spoof. There were five in the group, one of them was the compere and one got left out. His preferred method of editing would have been to cut it out with the cameras first time. Michael said to leave it to him.

Michael treated us just the same as *The Two Ronnies*, another of his many shows. But, of course, Ronnie Barker and Ronnie Corbett were two hugely experienced actors, while we were just a club act. We were instinctive performers used to reacting to things going wrong and lines being forgotten, especially by Syd. But that wasn't the BBC way. We had never sat down with a script and said, 'Right, you say that line and I'll say this one.' If we'd done that, Syd would have run from the room screaming. That was why Syd used to call me a one-man double act because often the comedy came from me improvising my way out of him getting something wrong. That was how the act formed. We didn't have a master plan.

Hurly-Burly was great at putting on the laughter track. He used to complain that we were talking over the laughs on his laughter track, we had to leave longer gaps. So much for comedy timing. We didn't even realise at first that a machine existed to inject false laughter. In the clubs, the audience soon told you if something wasn't funny.

Inside the studios, it was fun as well, largely because, perhaps to his credit, Michael Hurll didn't give a shit. You're absolutely not allowed to have animals in the BBC rehearsal rooms, but Hurly-Burly refused to let a little thing like a BBC rule get in the way of his genius. He had got this brilliant new idea that we would do sketches with animals and he had the poor dumb creatures smuggled up the back stairs.

We had a horse that could count, a *Mastermind* sketch with some penguins and some geese, and a giant pig that Syd tried to ride for some bizarre reason, which Norman Murray went mad about. 'Just do your act, Dolly,' he used to say. He didn't understand the need for all these crazy stunts, but they were often very funny.

In the final week of one series, Michael presented his *piece de resistance*... a kangaroo that was going to have a boxing match with Syd. We were intrigued by the idea and waited for the animal man, Bobby Roberts, to turn up. We were standing around the huge rehearsal room, which had a beautifully polished floor, talking about all the laughs we had enjoyed on the series, when this kangaroo burst in with Bobby Roberts hanging desperately onto its tail as if he were water-skiing. They were slipping all round the room at high speed, and Syd, Michael and I were crying with laughter as it just looked so funny.

When it came to the sketch at night, the audience hated the kangaroo because it battered Syd. You couldn't rehearse with a wild animal, so, once it had calmed down a little and had its boxing gloves put on, the kangaroo was brought face to face with Syd. There was a short puzzled pause as they looked at each other and then the kangaroo punched Syd. So he punched it back. That got a cheer. As a gag, we joked that they were cheering for the dumb animal. It was hilarious. Syd and the kangaroo went into this extraordinary fight routine that had to be seen to be believed.

Years later, they showed a bit on a documentary about Saturday-night television. Hurly-Burly said on the programme that it was the most politically incorrect sketch ever screened which was a bit rich as it was his idea. We never thought about that in those days, or how dangerous it was for poor Syd. The kangaroo had to have gloves on because they have claws like you wouldn't believe. If you're not careful, they can grab you with their front paws and disembowel you with their hind legs.

In the late 1970s, the line-up on BBC1 on Saturday night was *Jim'll Fix It*, *All Creatures Great and Small*, *Little and Large* and *Dallas*. The Texas soap was the biggy of the moment and JR Ewing was the king of television. We used to finish our show with me saying, 'Follow that, JR!'

When we were recording the last show of the series, we found that Larry Hagman, the man who played JR so brilliantly, was going to be in London. So I had the bright idea of having him come on after I said, 'Follow that, JR!' Everyone got very excited about this and messages were left everywhere for Larry Hagman to 'phone the *Little and Large* office'. This was on the Friday and we were due to record on the Sunday.

After we had finished for the day, the producer's PA offered to stay in the office in case Hagman telephoned. I got back to my home about 5.30pm and, half an hour later, I rang the office in my best Texan accent.

'Hi there,' I said. 'This is Larry Hagman calling.'

'Oh, Mr Hagman,' said the PA excitedly, 'thank you for calling.'

'I'd like to do the show,' I said.

'Oh, Mr Hagman,' said the PA. 'That would be wonderful. Little and Large will be thrilled.

'I like Little and Large,' I said, 'especially the Large one. He is so good at impressions.'

She volunteered, 'He is very talented.'

'He can even do me,' I said, 'and you would not know the difference.'

There was ten seconds of complete silence.

'You bastard, Eddie Large,' she said. 'I will never speak to you again.' She did, but she still has not quite forgiven me. Her name is Val Wilson and I would like to apologise again for the wind-up. Sorry, Val.

We did do some great sketches in our early days at the BBC. One of my favourites is Syd and I dressed as Andy Pandy and Noddy, and wired up to look as if we were puppets, singing a song that ended with us collapsing on to the floor on the line 'And we all fall down.' In rehearsal, we quickly discovered that the studio floor was very hard, so we asked Michael if we could use this bouncy castle-type thing from another sketch about space to land on. Michael Hurll saw the sense in that and it was blown up especially for us. After that, we did it in summer seasons and panto for years. A long time later, we would always flop down singing, 'And we all fall down,' and then look at each other and ask, 'How old are we?'

I used to pretend to get my leg caught in the wires as the sketch ended and people worried that I'd hurt myself. We did the Children's Royal Variety Performance and Princess Margaret was very concerned. Afterwards, she asked me, 'Was that very painful when you got your leg caught?' I couldn't bring myself to break it to her that I'd done it on purpose.

Frank Carson's technique for dealing with the public worked a treat. We were working on a Saturday on the BBC series and I asked Michael if I could leave early to go and watch Manchester City play at Birmingham. I was with a BBC journalist called Kevin Cosgrove who had done various TV interviews with us and was now making a documentary about City. We parked up and, as we walked to the match, I got the usual round of questions.

'Where's your mate?'

'Oh, he's in the boot looking after my golf clubs.'

'Eh, Eddie, where's Syd?'

'I've wrapped him round the steering wheel as a crook lock.'

'What's happened to Syd?'

'Oh, he's in the deep freeze. We're not working 'til nine so I won't defrost him until half-past eight.'

And so on and so.

Kevin was laughing away, thinking I was the wittiest person he'd ever met in his life. But, after the game, it was exactly the same routine.

'Where's Syd?'

'He's in the boot looking after my golf clubs…'

Kevin was stunned. 'I thought you were making that up as you went along.'

Sadly, it was all well rehearsed. You've got to have an answer ready otherwise you can appear rude and offhand. In the early days, the pressure from people did get to me at times, and Syd was brilliant at taking the heat off me. I always used to joke that he could talk to dead people. Syd can't ignore anyone; he'd be hopeless working in a bar.

Michael Barrymore was our warm-up man in the early days and he was very funny. One day, there was some technical hitch and he had to stay on much longer than he'd prepared so he started doing his act where he marches people out of the theatre. It was brilliant and he absolutely paralysed them. The audience was in hysterics and we couldn't follow them. Meanwhile, his wife Cheryl to see Michael Hurll, our producer, and said, 'That's what you want. Michael Barrymore, not Little and Large.'

Barrymore was so off the wall we couldn't understand his act at first. He used to pick on people and throw them out of the theatre. It was a strange technique. His aggression towards the audience really seemed to be against the grain. It takes some bottle and doesn't always work.

We were in Eastbourne with him once, which is not really Michael Barrymore country. He was doing his bit and the audience was fairly elderly, not really following what was going on too well. So Michael went into his John Cleese impression and started shouting, 'Right, you, out! This is not a gag. Get out.'

A fellow shakily stood to his feet and started to slowly walk towards the exit. His wife stood up and interrupted Michael and said, 'You'd better give him these,' holding up a pair of walking sticks.

To his credit, Michael waved the sticks and shouted, 'It's a miracle.'

Cheryl was a fabulous cook and we went to some marvellous dinner parties, but Syd and I were always annoyed that, in all his books and interviews, he never gave us any credit for the considerable amount of help and support we gave him in his early days.

Michael and Cheryl came to Dave's wedding, where Syd and I were joint best men. It was a great occasion, even if poor Dave did have to drive us from Bournemouth to Dundee the next day. But, according to Cheryl in her book, she was at the wedding and 'at my table was the comedian Eddie Large' as if we were not good friends. Then she wrote about Michael collapsing right into his meal, but as far as I can recall that simply never happened. But then, the Barrymores' behaviour was often bewildering. I was shocked when she died so suddenly.

Television was fun and on-screen success doesn't half work wonders on your live audiences. We travelled from Blackpool to Great Yarmouth with Frank Carson.

In his usual restrained manner, Frank had organised a Roller to take us. Syd and I would have been happy to go on the bus, but not Frank. He had to do everything in style.

So in 1978 we were in Great Yarmouth doing summer season with Frank Carson and Norman Collier. We did a record-breaking season of 100 full houses on the trot. You couldn't believe how well it was going. Somehow we never did become big-time, though. You hear about ludicrous demands of huge trailers and cars and so on but I'm pleased to say we never got into that. We had already recorded five shows of our new BBC series and we had started in Yarmouth before we had time to do the sixth show.

Every day I played golf with Frank and Norman. Tommy Cannon and Bobby Ball were there as well and often they would join in. Most of my memories are of laughter on the course. One day, Dave came to caddy because it was such lovely summer weather. In golf, if you hit a tree or something and it bounces back on the fairway they call it taking advantage of local knowledge. That was too long for Frank, who always abbreviates everything, so he shortened it to LK. Soon after we drove off he hit a shot into some trees and his ball hit a branch and bounced back on to the fairway. 'Ha, Ha,' chortles Frank, 'a bit of LK never fails.'

'What's that?' asks Dave.

'I said Local Knowledge,'

Dave snorted. 'Knowledge with a K,' he laughed.

I said, 'Ah well, Dave. You know Frank, he never could spell properly.'

Dave was not an educated guy and he made a lot of mistakes with his words but he was a lovely fellow and we never took the mickey cruelly. We were in a hotel one night and Brian used to like to do the crosswords. He was puzzled by the word ramrod. He asked me, 'Is there a hyphen in the word ramrod?'

'I don't think so,' I said cautiously, never too enthusiastic to commit myself in questions of spelling.

'I'm not sure,' said Brian. 'Isn't it unusual to have R following M in a word?'

'I suppose it is,' I said.

'Is it heck,' interrupted Dave. 'There's thousands of words with MR in them, Pengy,' he said. 'Isn't there, Ed?'

I hadn't a clue so I said I wasn't sure.

'There's hundreds anyway,' said Dave.

'Name me some of them then,' said Brian.

'Huh,' said Dave, 'Mr and Mrs.'

Syd and I fell about.

'No, no, no,' said Brian. But Dave was falling about laughing with me and Syd. He had no idea what was suddenly so funny but he liked the idea of a joke at Pengy's expense for once.

Showbusiness certainly opens some doors for you. In December 1978, we received an invitation from Prime Minister James Callaghan to a reception at 10 Downing Street. Dave drove us down and we had special permission to park in Downing Street. Going into Number 10 was amazing. It's huge inside and it opens up like the TARDIS. I couldn't believe it, but Dave refused to be impressed. I was marvelling while he brought me down to earth.

'It's only a council house like my mother's,' he snorted.

All good things come to an end and our professional relationship with Dave ended in typically hilarious fashion. We were in Wolverhampton and he'd just got married and had a baby, and he had a stepdaughter as well. Being a roadie is no job for someone with a new wife and a young family. Dave was also always arguing with Syd, which used to drive me absolutely crazy. With them being brothers, neither of them would ever give in and, of course, all the rows brought up ancient family disputes that you didn't want to know about.

I became close to Dave and whatever Ed said went. But Syd was going mad about Dave and, of course, as usual it was left to me to do something about it. We started using Dave after *Opportunity Knocks*: until then Syd was the best roadie I ever had but after people started to know us and ask us for autographs we couldn't really be lugging our amplifiers and stuff about ourselves. Dave was working on a building site then, so he wasn't making a huge amount of money.

He enjoyed the job and it worked well for a while but eventually the friction between Syd and Dave came to a head in Wolverhampton. There was a big row and Syd said, 'You've got to sack him.'

It was hard for Dave because he had a lot of pressure from home and we weren't that great to work for: we certainly weren't great payers! It came to a head and I had to say to Dave, 'Dave, you're sacked.' It might sound unlikely but his exact reply was 'Thanks very much.'

In the pub across the road, he got talking to some barrack-room lawyers and was soon back demanding redundancy. I had to explain, as kindly as I could manage, that the job was still open and he was being sacked, not made redundant. But we saw him all right and it was as much for his own good as ours. His rows with Syd were getting so bad that something would have snapped and he got a new job and was able to spend the sort of time he needed with his new family. We're still good friends to this day, I'm happy to say, and I always miss his unique sense of humour.

We hired a new roadie called Derek Whyborn. He was a terrific guy who had worked with the Black Abbots so he was very experienced. He was always very particular about making sure our clothes were clean and pressed and hung up, which was a totally new experience for us. We had always done all that sort of thing ourselves.

Derek had a way of making us laugh as well. When we were in Tenerife he knew he needed to hire an estate car, one big enough for all the gear. John, the compere, who spoke fluent Spanish, told him how to ask for it and Derek went off to organise the transport. But he came back and admitted that he was having trouble making himself understood. It turned out he was asking for an entrecote as John had thought he wanted the word for a steak.

Larry Grayson was in a rival show that summer at the Wellington and he had to be driven past our theatre every night in his Roller and see all the queues. He said to the head of the resort's entertainments people, 'I have seen people going in wearing jeans and shorts and trainers. We are going to get a better class of audience.'

I love Larry but that's a great illustration of how showbiz people always have to turn things round to their own advantage somehow: we might have got bigger crowds but his were better dressed!

We were having a great time. We used to go into a Greek restaurant every night where Norman Collier would cause mayhem.

One day, it was pelting down with rain so we couldn't play golf. What were we going to do? I was bored and then I thought, I know, I'll go and have my hair permed. It never occurred to me that we'd recorded five shows with my hair straight and then on a whim I had sent it all curly. Michael Hurll nearly collapsed when he saw me at the script conference. He went apeshit because he was busy mixing up all the shows, so I had to go back to the hairdresser and get it all straightened back again. It was a hell of a job.

Hurll's brain was brilliant. I didn't like him but he would give people a chance, as he did with our first production manager, Paul K Jackson, who he let direct and who subsequently rose to stardom. Another kid we had was Ed Bye, who is married to Ruby Wax and went on to become a great comedy director.

You could never work out Michael's love life. He was going out with a girl vision mixer who got pregnant and had a baby. Michael didn't tell anyone, and didn't know anyone knew, but in the gossipy BBC everyone knows everything. We were filming at a big store in Kingston and she came in with the baby and we were thrilled to see her and the new child. Everyone was cooing over the baby and Michael shooed her away. 'Do you mind, we're trying to film,' he said. He was a tough man.

The show was a success. The critics had a go but the public loved it. Bruce Forsyth had just changed channels to ITV and we were up against the hugely expensive *Brucie's Big Night Out* which had a massive budget and huge publicity. But we beat it in the ratings with our first series. We were quite chuffed to beat Bruce because to us he was like the king of variety at the time. Talk about being dropped in the deep end. We had done one series of television and suddenly we were in the frontline of the ratings battle. It was certainly a baptism of fire.

We had three years with Michael Hurll in charge and, after Michael left us to go on to other things, we took a little bit of a break for a couple of years. We got on with him OK but when he was working with us he was also doing *The Two Ronnies*, *Crackerjack* and *Top of the Pops*. Years later, he pronounced pompously on television that, if he was asked to replace Morecambe and Wise, he certainly wouldn't have picked Little and Large, but that is exactly what he did.

By that time, I don't think our television work was as good as it should have been. Jimmy Gilbert, the BBC's head of entertainment, took us out to lunch and I understand his brief was to talk about the declining quality of the comedy and to find out what was going wrong. But Jimmy was far too nice a person to discuss anything so confrontational and too much of a BBC executive to bother himself too much with programmes in detail, so it never came up. In our innocence we thought he just wanted to take us out for a meal so we never raised it. Then we did a special with Brian Penders and were given the experienced BBC producer Bill Wilson to guide us on to the screen.

We will both always be grateful to Bill Wilson. He came in and helped to give us a new lease of life. Bill was a wonderful man. He was the one who came in and made us rehearse. Hurly-Burly was not one for rehearsing. He would just leave us and expect us to do it on our own. When Bill arrived, it was completely different and we would rehearse everything. It raised the quality instantly, of course, and helped us enormously because we had the time to work out reactions and time our lines much better.

Great actors like David Jason and Ronnie Barker work like that and they are trained actors in the first place. We were a club act learning as we went along. If you get a laugh you pause, if you don't get a laugh you plough on. Actors know when to pause, but we didn't. Bill Wilson was a great guy to work with and he made us very conscious of leaving time for the laugh. If you watch David Jason in *Only Fools and Horses*, you can see he will pause and pull a face or give a look while the viewers are busy laughing.

Bill was so dedicated, and a lovely man. He may have got us rehearsing properly for the first time but it wasn't all hard work. I remember once at the famous Acton rehearsal rooms, in a break from going through our sketches, we were leaning out of the window on the fifth floor watching these cooling towers being painted.

The car park below was quite full and this little Mini drove in. I thought, He's going to have a struggle to park because we had trouble getting in earlier.

The Mini went into some extraordinary manoeuvres that had me and Syd fascinated. It started going backwards and forwards from the most eccentric angles. It seemed that there was just not enough space but, eventually, after performing a 33-point turn, the car finally made it into the single remaining empty parking space. We were in hysterics at these motoring antics as we gazed down from on high. And then we laughed even louder when the Mini's door opened and out stepped Spike Milligan. Of course, we realised it just couldn't have been anyone else. He is one of my all-time comedy heroes; he was better than wonderful that day.

People always think you have a hilarious time making a comedy show and sometimes you do, even if the funny moments are few and far between. One of the most memorable for me came when we were filming in Plymouth in 1990. We had been there since half-seven in the morning so, when it got past 9pm, we were more than a little tired. We were on Union Street, a bit of a notorious street for sailors and girls and the livelier kind of nightlife. We were outside a nightclub that was closed for the night and we were filming a sequence of busking sketches. The first one I think was 'On The Street Where We Live' with Syd playing the violin and then something would go wrong. The next one was 'Phantom of the Opera' and I had got the mask on. The third one is 'Cats' and we were dressed as two large moggies.

We were knackered, the crew was knackered and people were coming out of the pubs shouting at us and not always with messages of support. The gag was that we would go along the queue, as cats, singing 'Midnight...' and then someone would set all these dogs free. There were about 30 of them and they would chase after us and we had to dash round this corner. The dog owners didn't turn up until about nine o'clock and, of course, they were fresh as daisies, while we had been working hard all day. It was a little bit chaotic, with a Rottweiler determined to kill a poodle and one or two other unscripted canine clashes.

Syd and I were sitting around dressed as cats, desperate to get the whole thing over. Eventually, we settled down and did it. We rushed round the corner and Bill Wilson shouted, 'Cut.' Well, the dogs didn't understand 'Cut'. They were having a great time jumping up and snapping and biting at us. We were trying to fight them off until the owners arrived to grab them. It was chaos. And Bill decided we needed to do it again.

The dog owners were all giggling and laughing and excited at the prospect of getting their mutts on the telly, and we were heartily sick of the whole experience.

'Let's go again,' said Bill, and we dashed round the corner for the dogs to leap at us all over again. Some of them were really getting into the swing of it by now and being bitten was not fun.

We said, 'Is that it, Bill?'

'I'm sorry, boys,' he said. 'I just need to do it one more time.'

It was almost ten o'clock by then and the whole sketch was way past a joke for us. It was a low point for both of us. These cat suits were very thick so, on top of everything else, we were both boiling. A dog owner walked past us and said to Syd all soppy, 'I like your nose.' And Syd said, 'How would you like me to stick it up your ****ing arse.'

I just collapsed with laughter. I cried and cried with laughter for ages. And gradually it went round the crew what Syd had said and everyone was in hysterics. It was like a release at the end of a tough day and everyone was rolling around.

The funny thing was that it was such an un-Syd-like

thing to say. People might have expected me to say something rude like that, but not Syd. He was the nice guy, the quiet one who always stayed cool.

CHAPTER EIGHT

Leaving Auntie

We had lots of great guests on in our time on the box. Probably the best remembered was Cliff Richard. He always helped to guarantee big ratings and he was a remarkably nice fellow as well.

We had him on once and I pretended to kid Syd that it was tough to get guests on because they didn't want to compete and I did this really over-the-top impression of Cliff. I also pretended to be Englebert and then Lulu and the audience gradually got the idea that there was no big star, just me doing impressions. When Cliff came on for real, they loved it. He was behind me and I heard him laugh out loud as he came on. When they saw he was really there, the place went wild. I've never heard a studio audience react like that. It's a good job the show wasn't live because it would have overrun.

We had Status Quo on and they were all drunk out of their minds. We tried to do a little interview and they couldn't string two words together. They had a record out called 'Margarita Time'. The keyboard player Andy Bown came up to us and said, 'You're not going to get any sense out of them today. They've just had about 20 margaritas.' Francis Rossi and Rick Parfitt were always ones for giggling and that day they were uncontrollable.

Leslie Ash's younger sister Debbie had worked as a dancer with us earlier so we knew her well. We were down to appear on Noel Edmonds's *Multi-Coloured Swap Shop*, and she and Rick were in the audience. I plucked up courage to ask Rick if he would come on the show. He said, 'How could I turn down Syd and Eddie?' That took me back a bit and he explained. 'I was in a trio with two twin girls called the Hi-lites and we worked with you in Mr Smiths in Manchester. I can't refuse Syd and Eddie.'

We had The Shadows on and I did my version of Cliff with them and Syd even got to play his guitar with the world's most famous instrumental group. That was a major thrill for both of us. I really enjoyed myself and couldn't resist saying, 'Even Cliff Richard never got to sing in front of The Shadows and Syd Little.'

A lot of our dreams were realised through the business. I loved the early years of our flirtation with the pop world. Years after we had compered for The Searchers, they came on our tour to help us do a sketch. Similarly, we had introduced Gene Pitney on tour and were later able to invite him on to our very own show.

Of course, if you're appearing regularly on television, everyone thinks you are millionaires. Sadly, although you do make a good living, this is not true. And we also suffered financially because we had a dodgy accountant who died in 1986 and left us with a tax bill of close to £200,000. This guy borrowed money off us to pay his own tax and we lent it because he was a friend. We had a pension that was going to be worth half a million each and we'd be set up for life, or so we thought. But the accountant cocked it up. And, when you tell the story around, it seems to have happened to most people in showbusiness.

The divorce killed me financially as well. At the time, we were mega earners so that reflected the payments, and I was a softie and wanted the kids to be well provided for so I just let it go. And, of course, as the money declined, I was still paying at high rates.

It was hardly MY DRUGS HELL, as the tabloids might put it but I did take cocaine one night. It was definitely not planned and never repeated. Patsy and I used to live in Gerrards Cross, not far from Windsor where Syd and I had appeared earlier that evening at Blazer's Club. We had done our spot and for once I was not in a great hurry to get home as it's only a short taxi ride.

Syd, Dave and I were relaxing in the dressing room when this gangster-type guy came in and joined the chat. Conversations with strangers often happen and this bloke seemed fairly genial. Syd and Dave left to go back to their hotel. He said, 'Do you fancy some coke?'

I said, 'No, I'm happy with the champagne.' I was pretty clueless and embarrassed when he explained he was not talking about Coca-Cola. I was feeling pretty daring at the time or, to put it more accurately, pretty drunk. I am a bit straight-laced normally, to be honest, and if any of my kids did this I would go berserk, but I thought, Why don't I try it?

So this guy gets out this white powder and a £20 note and hands it to me and I sniff it. I got the taxi home soon afterwards and I confessed to Patsy what I had done. She had a go at me for being so stupid because we are both very anti-drugs. She said, 'That's it, you'll never get to sleep tonight, you'll be up all night.' But, in fact, I had one of the best nights' sleep I've ever had and I'm still waiting to feel the effect of cocaine. I don't think I'll try it again somehow. Whether it was a gag and he only gave me soap powder I'll never know but that is my one and only dabble in the drugs scene. It was pathetic.

Freddie Starr was one of my neighbours in those days, and knows about the tattoos I had done when I was a young man, something I've have regretted ever since. My father spent eight years in the navy and afterwards he was very proud that he had never been daft enough to have a tattoo done. But when I was growing up it was the thing to do, like it is again today among kids.

One night, Freddie said that he knew a way I could

have them removed – this is when it first came out about laser treatment. He said he would introduce me to a man who could take them all off quite painlessly, somewhere in Barking, Essex. I've never forgotten the night Freddie rang. *Cool Hand Luke* was on the telly again and I really wanted to get back to see that film and Patsy was out somewhere. I phoned this fellow but it was constantly engaged. So I phoned Freddie and explained that I couldn't get through. 'Come round,' said Freddie, all decisive. He gave me the directions to his house. It was called 'My Way'. Why wasn't I surprised by this?

Freddie was his usual irrepressible self, saying he's going to star in the next James Bond film. 'I'm going to see him tonight,' he said of the tattoo remover. 'I'm having one of mine done tonight. Do you want to come with me?' Freddie had a tattoo with the name of an ex-girlfriend and he wanted to get rid of it, for obvious reasons. He had actually been trying to get rid of this particular tattoo for years. He once poured sulphuric acid on to it. He told me about the experience, jumping over sofas like a kid to show me how he reacted to the pain and, of course, I was laughing, but in spite of all that I said, 'All right.'

We jumped into Freddie's car and, after calling in at the Hilton, where Freddie bought some jewellery, eventually we got to the guy's place in Barking. We went in and I asked Freddie, 'Are you having yours done?'

'Y-Y-You go first,' said Freddie. 'I'm working tonight at the Circus Tavern.'

I said, 'All right, I'll have it done.'

The whole treatment was in its very early stages, but anything to get rid of those tattoos. He injected adrenaline right into the skin where the tattoos were so I wouldn't feel the pain. It was agony. I learned later this guy had been a doctor but he had been struck off. Freddie, who wasn't working at all, was pissing himself. They had a fan to take the smell of the burning flesh away. It didn't hurt particularly but it gave me a third-degree burn. The laser evaporates the ink and that burns away the flesh with tattoos on. There was nothing magical about it.

Afterwards they gave me loads of dressings and antiseptic stuff. Freddie was still pissing himself. Eventually he drove me home. I'd left a note for Patsy: 'Just going with Freddie to get my tattoos removed,' so naturally she was terrified because I was with him.

When she saw the treatment I'd had from the tattoo remover, Patsy was absolutely horrified. The guy said I had to keep the dressings on for a couple of days, by which time we were working in Birmingham. When I took the dressings off, it was all infected. I had serious burns and I was in agony, and it's amazing how many people touch you on the arm. I kept leaping up and down screaming every time anyone came near to me.

It didn't make any difference to the tattoos at all. Mercifully, they have faded naturally over the years. This remover was a bit of a rogue who was not properly qualified. Esther Rantzen rang me up, wanting to expose him by showing a video she had received of me having my treatment, but I was too embarrassed to admit it was me.

To Freddie, it was one of the funniest days of his life. He just enjoyed me being in absolute agony. He is one of the best entertainers in Britain, and when he tells you about pouring acid over his own tattoos he has you crying with laughter, but he does have a cruel streak running through him.

Patsy doesn't know any golfers. She is just not interested. For years, the height of my ambition wasn't being plucked to international stardom in Las Vegas but getting chosen to appear on BBC2's *Pro-Celebrity Golf*. I loved that programme and I love golf.

In 1985, the magic letter arrived. The BBC would like you to appear on... 'Oh yes!' I yelled out loud. It was two days up in Turnberry and I could take Patsy and our two-year-old son Ryan. We were doing a tour at the time but I was much more concerned with finding out which top golfer I would get the chance to play with. I kept asking Patsy if the BBC had been on with any more details, as I was so impatient to find out.

Finally, the vital call came. 'The BBC have been on,' Patsy told me. 'You'll never guess who you're playing with in the *Pro-Celebrity Golf*.'

'Yes, who?'

'Mike Reid!'

'Yes, Mike Reid. I know him very well but who is the golfer.'

'It'll be fantastic,' said Patsy. 'We'll be up there for a couple of days so we can have dinner with Mike and Shirley.'

'Yes, Patsy, but what about the professionals?'

'Arnold someone and someone Player… I think,' said Patsy. You'd almost think she was deliberately trying to wind me up.

'Arnold Palmer and Gary Player!'

'Yes, I think so,' said Patsy. 'But isn't it great that we'll be able to have dinner with Mike and Shirley.'

What can you say? I couldn't care less about playing Mike Reid. We've played together loads of times and we're mates, but to be on the same course as two of the greatest golfers who have ever swung a club was absolutely amazing to me. It still is, all these years later. They were both magnificent. Arnold Palmer came up to me and said, 'I'm Arnold Palmer, you must be Eddie.' I almost fainted. Arnold Palmer was explaining who *he* was to me.

I used to argue with Bill Wilson that we should have the same sorts of things in the same section every week and he would always insist that we made it different. Now *The Fast Show* does exactly that sort of comedy by familiarity: 'Suits you, sir,' becomes funny because it's repeated. But we were never allowed to go down that route. Bill had bosses who liked it that way at that time, and that was the trouble at the BBC, you weren't really doing shows for the viewers, you were doing them for BBC bosses, most of whom you never got to meet.

The end with the BBC was quite strange – it might be known by some as 'Auntie', but they didn't treat us like family. They didn't even say we were being sacked. We were invited to the Savoy along with our agent Peter Pritchard. BBC comedy kings Jimmy Moir, John Howard Davies and John Bishop were also there. Jimmy was a great bloke. For the first time in our lives, we had wine with the starter, wine with the sorbet, wine with the main course. One of the BBC executives was a big expert. Knowing the BBC, he was probably Head of Wine.

Jimmy presented us with two huge goblets, one inscribed with S, the other with E. There was no word that we had been sacked but the months went on and there was no news on another series.

Peter Pritchard phoned up and said, 'Very funny thing, guv'nor. Did you know you've got the sack from the BBC?'

I said, 'Yes,' although I didn't really know any such thing.

'Well, they've had a meeting and Little and Large is the top-rated light entertainment show in the ratings so one of the BBC governors said, "Well I'm glad we've got Little and Large."'

But they didn't, because they had sacked us. So Jimmy's boss said you'd better get Little and Large back and Jimmy said, 'Well you'd better phone Peter Pritchard because I'm not doing it.' So we did one more series because of that.

By the time we came to the last series, I'd had enough because the political correctness was just getting ridiculous. We did a sketch with Maria Whittaker, a Page 3 girl, and we were dancing round this May Pole to the 'Day I Went To Bangor' song. Syd is the Maypole. We were doing lots of old jokes and had tied Syd up with the ribbons.

And Syd said to me, 'Where are you going now?'

And I said, 'I'm just taking her to Bangor.'

Bill Wilson said, 'No.'

'What's wrong?'

'You can't say that.'

'Why not?'

'You know why not.'

We argued but I thought the line was fair enough.

Maria said, 'I don't understand what you're on about. I don't get it.' I thought that rather made my point. It was the sort of double entendre that the young and innocent would miss altogether. But we couldn't use it. I thought it was ridiculous then, and nowadays it seems even more ridiculous.

Bill was a good man but he was BBC through and through. There are far too many programmes made for those bosses upstairs.

Anne Robinson was the straw that broke the camel's back. Well, she certainly looks like a camel anyway.

She was presenting the BBC's *Points Of View* programme when we filmed a sketch featuring me as an ice-cream man and Syd as a punter. The joke was that Syd comes up, orders an ice cream and, when he turns round, there's a little kid looking wide eyed at the ice cream. So Syd gives him the ice cream. Another little kid does the same thing. In the end, Syd buys ice creams for a succession of seven kids, who are all in on the scam. Then the mother of the kids comes out and says, 'Say goodbye to your father, kids.' And, as the ice cream man, I say 'Goodbye' to them. I'm their father and the joke is that Syd's been tricked into buying seven ice creams.

We played it back to the audience, and our rule was, if it doesn't get a laugh in the studio, it doesn't go in the show. It got a big laugh.

Before the recording we had our meeting and I said, 'Bill, we've got to be careful about this one because we've got kids taking ice creams from a stranger.'

We thought about it and decided it was fair enough and it was funny: the mother and father were both there so there's no danger of the stranger enticing the kids. So it went in the show. After transmission, *Points Of View* phoned our office to say they'd had loads of complaints, and in their next edition Anne Robinson really went for us. I thought then that it was not fair, and I still think it today.

Of course, being the BBC's own programme, *Points Of View* carried a great deal of weight. But we weren't being irresponsible. Whatever you do can be misinterpreted, if someone is really determined to take offence. We got a lot of criticism and we took it, but when it is unfair you think, Why should we carry on taking it? That was a sketch we had really thought about and the criticism from Anne Robinson and *Points Of View* really knocked the stuffing out of us a bit. It became ridiculous.

We took a lot of stick from the critics in our time and not all of it was justified. Much more recently, I was a team captain on a show called *Gag Tag* and I was much heartened when Jonathon Ross remembered some of our routines with great affection. 'You did some good stuff,' he said. 'But you didn't half get some stick from the critics.'

He was right. One of our worst attackers was Nina Myskow, who got very personal in some of her attacks. She was writing, if that's not too strong a word, for the *News of the World*. The first show came out on a Saturday and predictably she slagged us off. It was just what we expected but, when I read it for a second time, I noticed that she had not really pinpointed anything about the show. She did not describe a particular sketch or song.

I phoned our press agent, George Bartram, and asked why she had not criticised any item in the actual show. George explained to me that she had not seen the show. He said her page was completed long before Saturday night and no advance tape had been available. George said he complained but nothing ever came out about it. I just thought it was unfair to have a go when you haven't even seen the show. And all these years later I still feel like that. Nina was not one of our favourite people.

I'm not bitter about the way things have changed, I just wish people would show a little more respect publicly. A lot of the younger comics do privately. We have been on with Vic Reeves and Bob Mortimer and they remembered lots of our sketches very fondly. But to say they like Little and Large is an unfashionable thing to come out with. I know for a fact that Ben Elton likes Bernard Manning. Some of Bernard's material might be indefensible but he is a great comic.

One of the best-remembered pieces of TV I was involved in was when Noel Edmonds dressed up as a gorilla to deliver one of his Gotcha awards to me. People seemed surprised that I kept my temper throughout a long and totally convincing wind-up to the gag and I certainly came close to losing it. But you learn to live with being part of public property. It goes with the territory.

I have always liked Noel Edmonds. He was a great professional, who put together some big shows and presented them very well. Whenever we worked with him, he never seemed to use the autocue, which is pretty rare in my experience. I was impressed by him.

Some time earlier, we had appeared on *Noel's House Party*. We were chatting to Noel and his producer Mike

Leggo, who had worked on our show, about a time I was driving from Bristol to the Isle of Wight and almost lost my temper with another driver. We all laughed, but Mike and Noel put that away in their mental filing cabinets for future use, noting that I had a temper to lose, and this whole Gotcha was created to wind me up.

Syd dragged me into a meeting with a reporter that I definitely didn't want to do. I was busy and irritable before we started, and then the wind-up began. It was 1993 in Torquay and I should have been playing golf. He got our agent Peter Pritchard to help persuade me so I agreed.

I wandered into this hotel all scruffy, as if I was going to play golf, but the girl reporter was quite attractive, so to my eternal shame I started flicking my hair into place to try and make myself look more presentable. Only I was looking into a mirror which, unknown to me, had a camera behind it! The wind-up started and, although it did get me annoyed, we've been through it all before so I did have an answer. But by the time a birthday cake arrived and this gorilla started pulling it to bits, I was ready to blow. Fortunately, just in time, Noel, who was in the gorilla suit, dug the golden Gotcha statuette out of the cake and gave it to me, and I realised I had been well and truly had!

It was brilliant, even if I was the butt of the joke.

Fame is a strange thing to deal with. When we were up there at the top, I always tried hard never to let it go to my head, but sometimes it has an effect on those around us.

One of my oldest mates is a guy called Jimmy Brown. As young men, we had been in many Indian restaurants together, and very often, when we'd had a few, we would try to dash out without paying. It was just one of the crazy things that teenagers do.

Years later, we caught up with him again, by which time Syd and I were doing quite well. He came to see us and we all went for a curry somewhere in Stockport. We were following him as he parked outside a restaurant, but then drove off and parked outside another one. We asked why he didn't want to stop at the first restaurant, and he said, 'I didn't think it was good enough for you two.'

I was a bit hurt that he thought of us in a different way but I suppose it's inevitable. But Syd and I both tried hard not to get grand or big-headed, and to always stay in touch with our roots. I reckon if you forget where you've come from you could soon lose sight of where you're going, if that's not too corny.

It was the same with my sister. We didn't communicate for years, but for what reason I have no idea, and then she came to see us in Blackpool in 1992 and we went over the road and had a wonderful chat. It was just like the old days as we talked all about the kids and the family and everything. Afterwards, she wrote me this really poignant letter about how they thought they were not good enough for me now I was on television. It was heart-rending and I was really upset.

She was a really quiet little girl but she ran the only drug-free pub in Wythenshawe for a time. I used to go and watch City playing and these guys would come up to me saying, 'I've tried to get in your kid's pub but she's barred me.' I used to get that wherever I went but there was nothing I could do to help. Irene ran the place with a rod of iron.

I am amazed and very proud at how my brother and sister have done. I suppose being the oldest child and the head of the family and having done well in showbusiness, maybe I was so bound up in my own concerns and ambitions that I didn't give that much time to what my brother and sister were doing, but they've done well and that's brilliant.

Happily, we have kept much more in touch since and we are quite close now, but families are funny things. My brother and my sister both call me Edward and to this day they like to ask Patsy if she has got any Blue Ribands in for me, the nice chocolate bars that my mother always used to make sure she had when I called at home after being away. Irene and Brian both take the mickey: Edward's coming home, get in some Blue Riband.

A particularly tough year was 1986. It was the year my parents died. Patsy was pregnant and lost the baby. The year before, my mother was in hospital in Wythenshawe, unhappy in this particular ward. We visited on a really snowy day. She was 70 years old and still very alive and alert but she definitely didn't like this ward. My dad said, 'Oh she'll be all right.' But my mother was not all right.

When we arrived, she had a very curious complaint. 'That bloody monkey out there keeps looking at me,' she said.

My dad said, 'Oh yes, Jessie, we'll get it sorted out,' suggesting that her mind was perhaps beginning to go a little.

But I wasn't happy with that. I tried to assure my mum that there was no monkey out there in snowy Wythenshawe; it was brass monkey weather if anything. But my mother insisted and I was worried, seriously concerned about her mental state. A couple of days later, we went back to see her and she seemed a little better in herself. We were all more relaxed and then I glanced out of the window and got quite a shock – there *was* a monkey. Actually, it was a weird crossover of drainpipes on a wall that formed a clear and distinct monkey silhouette. I shouted, 'Hey, there *is* a monkey out here.'

My dad said, 'Don't you start.' But I was able to show them and after that it became a family joke.

But the death of my parents highlighted a very cruel side of showbusiness. 'There's no business like showbusiness, we smile when we are low…' goes the old song, and it is so true. In January 1986, my dad was very ill. Syd and I were at the Wolverhampton Grand doing panto. Patsy and I drove up to Manchester where we were told he was not going to last the night, but he did, so we went back to Wolverhampton and did the show. Then we went back to the hospital where the same thing happened again.

Next day, we went back and booked into a hotel near the hospital. We got a call, which said, 'Your dad is slipping away,' so, of course, we rushed over, but this time Teddy had passed away. Nothing prepares you for the feeling of losing someone you love, and as everyone knows you just have to try to get through it as best you can. But not everyone has to go on stage and try to be funny immediately afterwards and that's why, in my humble opinion, showbusiness is a little bit different.

Back at the Grand, one of the features of the show was that we had some very enthusiastic junior dance teams who kept asking for messages to be read out for each other. 'The red team wants to wish the yellow team all the best.' I was moaning to Syd that we ought to cut this out because it was slowing down the show.

I had returned from the hospital full of emotion about my father and was in the dressing room trying to prepare for the show when there was a knock on the door. Some of the child dancers were there and I knew they would have some new request and everything welled up inside me. I was just about to deliver a really angry earful when a little lad held up a card and said, 'We're sorry to hear about your father.' I felt terrible. I really felt awful, as I was just about to give them a blast.

Thank goodness for once I kept my mouth shut just long enough.

On 2 June, I received a call from my brother to say our mum was bad. I drove straight up to Wythenshawe Hospital and she didn't seem too bad at all. I was surprised and delighted. It was our Alison's 13th birthday and after visiting mum I drove off to Bury to surprise her as she got off the school bus, and after giving her a card and a present I headed off back home to Bristol. Just as I arrived, the phone rang: it was my brother Brian saying that Mum was not going to last the night.

I arrived back in Manchester in the early hours of the morning to find Brian cracked up in the corridor. 'She's gone,' he said grimly.

I missed it. I felt awful, but then almost straight away the job loomed up. I cancelled that night's show but we were on tour and you just can't let down all those people.

The funeral was set for the following Thursday. The night before, we were in Weymouth. I drove back to Bristol to pick up Patsy, went up to Manchester for the funeral, then back to Bristol to drop off Patsy and on to Walthamstow where we did two shows in the town hall and a charity night at La Taverna in Epping. It's hard to cancel things like that, even if you do have powerful personal reasons, because it always means letting so many people down.

Afterwards, I was just totally exhausted, sitting in the dressing room feeling desperately sad that I couldn't even begin to grieve properly, when in walked someone I won't name who said cheerily, 'You're not as good as you used to be.' For once I didn't react. I just sat with my head in my hands and thought what a perfect end to a bloody awful day.

Tragically, that was not the end of our awful news. The third dreadful heartbreak came when Patsy lost our baby. She had been pregnant for five months and the loss was almost too hard to bear.

I am a pretty optimistic guy by nature but that year it was desperately hard to look on the bright side of anything. Patsy and I were so happy when she became pregnant. Ryan was just four years old then and we had always dreamed of him having a little brother or sister. Of course, we just wanted a healthy baby, but a little daughter would have been perfect.

The pregnancy felt like some sort of compensation for losing my mum and dad. I had lost two people who were so close to me, but we had been given the baby we wanted. It felt as if the scales of justice were weighing things up for us and we were both over the moon. Patsy did not feel very well throughout the pregnancy. She did not think it was anything unusual, as she had felt pretty rotten when she was carrying Ryan. We were just so happy we never thought anything could go wrong.

I remember in detail the day it happened. We went to the funeral of the first wife of the showbusiness manager John Miles. We came back from the funeral and Patsy began having terrible pains. We called the doctor who immediately sent her to hospital. They rushed her into the emergency department and gave her drugs to help relieve the pain. It was a terrible experience for Patsy.

Miscarrying at that late stage is like having a baby. Poor Patsy had to go into labour knowing that our baby was dead. It was the worst thing I've ever experienced in my life. Patsy was unbelievably brave and strong.

I insisted that the doctor told us what sex the baby was. He didn't want to tell us but I kept on at him and eventually he told me it was a girl. I just totally cracked up then because that is just what we wanted to make us the perfect family.

It was very hard to get over the ordeal. Everyone noticed Patsy had gone from being blooming and pregnant to being suddenly slim again but no one knew what to say. In the end, there is nothing you can say. You find everywhere you look there are reminders of babies. Ryan was a real tower of strength to us both through all this. I don't know what we would have done without him. He had been really looking forward to having a baby sister. He kept saying, 'I want a gril,' which was the nearest he got to 'girl'. He couldn't understand what had happened and kept asking why. And that was unanswerable. Some friends and family urged us to try again, but we couldn't bear the thought of going through that again.

In search of some consolation, perhaps, some time afterwards, I went to see the famous spiritualist Doris

Stokes. I'm the most cynical person I know, but I went. I had a guilt complex about my parents dying. I felt terrible because I was always on the road and there were so many things I should have done for them but there never seemed to be the time and you always put those sorts of things off. I would go up to a match and pop in afterwards, then I'd be rushing off out again. I never found the time, which I will always regret.

I went to see Doris in Lewisham and, as soon as I arrived, her husband got up and went out to walk the dog. Doris was like your favourite auntie, all pink and plump with loads of cakes on doilies.

'I've got your mother,' she said.

I am Mr Unbeliever, but I wanted to believe her because I'd heard her on the radio.

'Your mother is glad she went before she had to go under the knife.'

I thought, If that was a guess it's a cracker, because my mother had gangrene in her leg and was terrified of the operation.

Then Doris said, 'I've got your father here. No, I can't say that. No, I can't possibly say that.'

I am on the edge of my seat by this point, thinking what on earth is she hearing that is too bad to say? She said she couldn't tell me, but I said I didn't mind. I knew how belligerent my dad could be.

Doris relaxed a little and said, 'Well, he said you're a lazy bugger just like that other lazy bugger you work with.'

I was stunned. It might not sound much but it is exactly the sort of thing my dad would have said. Then she described our house where we used to live and how Patsy and I lost a baby. It was a brilliant experience. It felt almost cleansing, really. I drove back home from Lewisham and I felt fantastic.

CHAPTER NINE

The Beginning Of The End

Peter Kay certainly provided the highlight of 2005's Comic Relief effort with his hilarious 'Is This the Way to Amarillo?' video. It was a brilliantly simple and effective routine and I'm still disappointed not to have been a part of it.

Little and Large were asked to join in and it would have been enormous fun as well as a chance to help a very good cause. But my partner – or should I say *former* partner – Syd Little declined to take part. We have not spoken face to face about his decision but I was told he no longer wishes to work with me. I was saddened and disappointed that after all these years we couldn't at least have a chat about the situation between us. But I was not surprised. Syd is not very good at dealing with anything face to face.

I was hurt and angered by the suggestions in his autobiography that I had behaved badly towards him during our long partnership. He accused me of bullying him, which was a surprise to me. Perhaps I was a little forceful from time to time, but one of us had to take some responsibility and it certainly wasn't going to be Syd. If bullying is standing up for yourself, which I've had to do for 40 years, then that's all right. But he went on to accuse me of driving him to a heart attack, which was simply untrue.

I reacted to that accusation by complaining to Syd's ghostwriter. Syd is entitled to his opinion of me, certainly, but that's not the way it happened. At least now I know the act is over. I just wish Syd for once had found the bottle to tell me straight.

In our time together, quite a lot of the real personalities of Little and Large came out on stage. When I was a teenager in the gang, I was always the clown. Syd was a real-life straight man in a way. When I first met him, all his mates used to take the mickey out of him about being thin. He was just the fall guy. If there was a fight, Syd would be standing to one side holding the coats. Inevitably, I would be in the middle of it.

Syd has a way of never being responsible for anything. Why did you move to Torquay? It wasn't my idea. Why did you buy a B&B? It wasn't my idea. He can also be quite secretive. He swore our accountant to secrecy as far as I was concerned because he knew I would have advised him against going into a business he knew nothing about. He was quite lucky to sell it in the end.

Lots of times people told me I should get rid of Syd and go on my own, but I was happy with what I was doing. I didn't expect us to attain the heights we did but I had faith in us as an act. We had watched acts come to clubs and do cross patter and they had died on their arses. It was difficult to get the drinkers' attention. If you see the comedians from the 1970s like Frank Carson he is firing a machine gun of gags. Jack Benny used to love loads of long pauses but he never worked the northern clubs. Bobby Ball is on the attack as soon as he comes on.

I remember Eric Morecambe saying he watched some acts that were actually learning as they went along, and he was dead right. Morecambe and Wise came from theatre and they had the experience to time gags because the audience was sitting in rows listening, not sitting at tables drinking. Morecambe and Wise were never comfortable in clubs. I saw Eric and Ernie at a club in the north and it didn't go well.

Syd is basically a nice lad but, like me and everyone else, he is not without faults. He is the master at getting people to feel sorry for him. I used to call him the master of self-delusion. A couple of years ago, we were doing a tour of holiday camps and he annoyed me. Derek was driving us around and Syd said, 'Of course, he [meaning me] never came to my wedding.'

'Oh, didn't you, Mr Large?' sparks up Derek. 'Why was that then?'

I thought, he's done it again. Derek's feeling sorry for him. We all went to sleep in the caravan and when we woke up I had a real go at Syd. I said, 'You know perfectly well the reason I didn't go to your wedding.'

'Well, you didn't, did you?'

I said, 'No, but I'll tell you why, shall I?' and as soon as I say that he starts to shit himself, because the truth is Syd does make you laugh doing some very un-Syd-like things.

We were in Bristol in January 1975, down the bill. Dora Bryan was top of the bill, and Norman Vaughan and Mark Wynter were there too. Syd was with his present wife, Sheree, and they were staying about eight miles outside Bristol at some farm. There was also an acrobatic team on, Johnny Hutch's Half-Wits. They were all young lads and there was me and Dave the roadie and some dancers who all used to go to the pub over the road from the stage door. We were all having a laugh and went on to Hickey's nightclub.

Next day, I could see Syd was bridling a bit at all the talk of the great night out we'd had, because he'd always gone back to Sheree, as they were like an old married couple. As the pantomime was going on, everyone teamed up, including me with a girl called Jean who I was very fond of at the time. Even Dave had a girlfriend in the show.

Syd got the word that one of the dancers in the show

fancied him, which we all thought was hilarious because even his best friend wouldn't rate Syd highly in the pulling stakes. And, anyway, he was with Sheree now, and we're talking John and Yoko here. One night there was a party at the house of one of the dancers, and Sheree, never really a drinker, collapsed completely drunk and out of it, and Syd was with the dancer who fancied him giving it the old big lips.

We couldn't believe what we were seeing. We were all pissing ourselves because this behaviour was so unlike Syd. He and Sheree were so devoted, and still are to this day. Me and Dave were killing ourselves laughing because Syd is not famous as a passionate guy.

The next day was Sunday, a day off, and we all went home. On Monday morning, we all returned and Syd was on his own. Me and Dave couldn't believe our eyes. In the first place the arrival of Sheree actually threatened our relationship because me, Dave and Syd were three lads together, chatting the girls up, doing the dirty jokes and generally having a laugh. Then all of a sudden Yoko's there. It was the same scenario as The Beatles. They were just a little bit more successful. But it was just as traumatic for me as it was for Paul, George and Ringo. We used to come back from the matinee on a Saturday afternoon desperate to watch the football results and Sheree would be sitting there watching *The Thorn Birds* or a film. It is only a small thing, I know, but this caused a lot of tension between Syd and I and sparked a lot of fallouts.

So this Monday, when we thought they had gone back to arrange the wedding, Syd returned on his own. 'Where's Sheree?' we asked.

'The wedding's off,' said Syd with a face like thunder.

We couldn't take this seriously at first and Dave and I were laughing because again this was so un-Syd-like.

'What do you mean the wedding's off?'

'I'm not ready to get married again,' said Syd. So that was it. Sheree was history and the wedding was off.

Meantime, I booked a holiday for the time we'd left free for the wedding. It was a week in Tenerife, the first time I'd ever been there. Syd teamed up with this young dancer and it was all change as she moved into the farm that Sheree had moved out of. When the pantomime finished, Syd moved back to his mother's because he had been staying with Sheree's family. As there was no central heating, I was thinking, He won't survive that, and, like many pantomime romances, once the run finished, so did the romance.

Slowly and surely, Syd got back with Sheree, but no one told me. There was a lot of tension between us at that time. After a run at a nightclub in Charnock Richard, we were just finishing a meal and the waiter said, 'See you in a few weeks, then.'

'No, I don't think so,' I said, knowing we had no plans to come back soon.

'Oh,' he said, 'you know, for Syd's wedding. The reception is here.'

I was furious. The old Scottish temper was roused

and we went out into the car park. Dave knew but hadn't told me, so I thought, being dramatic, that he'd betrayed me. Syd and I had a massive row. I felt really let down that Syd hadn't seen fit to tell me about his rearranged wedding. It felt like I'd been stabbed in the back and I told Syd the act was finished.

Next day, our manager Brian Hart, who could see his commission going out of the window, called us to a meeting and we decided to keep going, though the atmosphere was far from friendly. The following Tuesday, Dave and I went to our next booking, in Eastbourne, in one car, Syd in another. When we arrived we were shown to the chalet where they used to accommodate the entertainers – the three of us. There was still a lot of tension between us but we went on that night and did well.

Next day, we woke up and Syd had gone, probably shopping. Dave and I decided to go and have a walk round Tunbridge Wells. We were just ambling around killing time when who should we see coming in the opposite direction but Syd and the dancer he'd gone off with. To us, it was funny because this behaviour was just so unlike Syd. We were crying with laughter at the very idea of Syd the great seducer. Next thing was he moved out of our chalet and into another one with the dancer. We continued until the Saturday and then he went back home, and he proceeded to get married to Sheree and live happily ever after.

It's a joke to compare Sheree to Yoko and us to The Beatles. Honest. Even in my most deluded moments I don't consider we're remotely similar. But our act was never quite the same after Sheree came on the scene. They were inseparable and it began to annoy me that the act no longer seemed the same. We'd sing "Til There Was You' and he would be looking at Sheree like a lovestruck teenager instead of concentrating on our act.

The performance meant everything to me and Syd's behaviour did upset me. I don't think Syd ever felt the same way about the work we were doing, although he enjoyed the money in our heyday. A reporter asked him once in an interview if he was allergic to anything and he replied, 'Yes. Showbusiness.'

I suppose we were like chalk and cheese but a lot of double acts are like that. It's great when you're successful, as you can lead separate lives because you have the money to do it.

Now Syd is a Christian, he has erased things like that from his memory bank. Derek and I always used to say that Syd has a brain like a video recorder. He cuts out things he doesn't want to remember and it is as if they have never happened. And Syd does have his own unique way of rewriting history. He had a heart attack in February 1993 and, years afterwards, he decided it was my fault because of all the pressure I had been putting on him. I was hurt by this allegation because it simply wasn't true.

But I keep diaries and I went back to them to recall

what really happened. It was on Sunday, 7 February 1993 when Sheree telephoned me to say that Syd had suffered a heart attack. Naturally, I was very concerned but she was quick to assure me it was only a mild one and he would only be in hospital for a few days.

Patsy was shocked by the news but, to be honest, I was not. The previous weekend had been difficult. We were flying to Belfast to appear on the *Kelly Show*, a late-night chat programme, so Syd drove from Torquay to pick me up at my home near Bristol and then on to Birmingham Airport. On the same flight was an old pal who was also on the show, Alan Randall, famous for his impersonations of George Formby. Manfred Mann and the brilliant guitarist Gordon Giltrap were also in the line-up.

After the show, we all ended up in the bar at the hotel. I could no longer take the long drinking sessions like I used to, so I left Syd and the rest of them to it and went to bed at about 1am. I had been warned to take it easy on the drinking when I had my pacemaker fitted in 1991.

Next morning we were on the early flight back to Birmingham and, as soon as I saw Syd, I knew he had been overindulging. I asked him what time he got to bed and he mumbled that it had been 3 or 4am and he was still drunk. When we got back to Birmingham, he was still in such a state that I had to drive us to Northampton, where we were appearing in cabaret at the Saxon Hotel. We had a couple of rooms booked so I left Syd to sleep it off. Our roadie Derek arrived with my suit at around five o'clock. He had just seen Syd and wanted to know what was wrong with him so I explained about the night before. Derek was a non-drinker and he definitely didn't approve of Syd's excessive drinking. After all, he was the one who had to put Syd to bed when he was out of it.

That night on stage, Syd was all over the place. He's been singing 'Ruby, Don't Take Your Love to Town' for about 30 years but he forgot all the words, which didn't help my interjections. It was a disaster. Our act might have been built on Syd getting things wrong and me making a joke of it, but this was taking things way too far. It was our worst performance ever. I don't know if this was the beginning of his heart attack, but that night we died on our arses. Afterwards, I didn't say anything. There was no point: he knew perfectly well that it had not been his best performance and he drove me back to Bristol the next day in silence. So the following day when I took the call from Sheree I was not in the least surprised.

The next year, Syd got the wrong end of the stick in a big way when he thought I had decided we were splitting up. All his life he has cried poverty, saying he's never got any money and we're not got going to get any more work. He has always been a worrier. I remember, in 1994, Derek said to me, 'Syd's buying Sheree a Merc.'

I said, 'He can't be. He's broke.'

He hadn't told me and I felt a bit put out that this man who had been moaning to me that he had no money was suddenly buying his wife a Mercedes. I tackled him and we had a bit of a row, and then afterwards I thought, I was out of order there. It's nothing to do with me whether or not he's buying a Merc. I shouldn't have done that.

Instead of confronting him again, because I know better than anyone that he hates any face-to-face stuff, I wrote to him to apologise. I explained that, at the time, I was under financial strain, as the maintenance payments were high, and I needed to do more of my after-dinner speaking to get some money together. The after-dinners are something I enjoy and, as I do them alone, they can be a handy source of extra income. I didn't want us to split up, and I didn't write anything about us splitting up, but that was how he interpreted it.

Every time I tell Syd I was talking to his brother he moans instantly, 'He never phones me.' But there was always a lot of rivalry between Syd and Dave. Syd didn't go to his 50th birthday party and I don't think Dave will ever forgive him. It was in Sale Town Hall near where Dave's twin sister lives. Dave lives in Bournemouth and came up with his son Richard, and his older brother Peter and family came up from Nottingham. I drove Patsy and Ryan up from Bristol.

'Where's Syd?' I asked, although I knew he wasn't coming. He was only in Blackpool but he chose not to attend. I tried to defend him as usual by saying he had arranged to do a charity function: he told me he wasn't coming because some friends had bought tickets for them to go to a charity dinner dance and he didn't want to let their friends down, which to me seemed a feeble excuse for not attending his brother and sister's 50th. Dave was going mad and Peter was absolutely seething. Syd was the most hated man on the planet that night. I thought it was just sibling rivalry but maybe there was something deeper between them.

In 2000, we were due to do a summer season in Jersey. We were booked Monday, Tuesday and Wednesday for ten weeks, and Billy Pierce was doing the other days. Billy went to Jersey to check things over and he came back insisting that the venue was not going to be ready, so the booking went belly-up and we had a big hole in our summer work. We had some other dates but we were without a summer season. At home, Syd made himself busy painting a wall at his son Dominic's school and, according to Syd, one of the women at the school phoned the press. He rang me at home in a panic because a reporter and a photographer had turned up. He said, 'They want to do a story about me going back to decorating. What do you think?'

I said, 'If you don't co-operate they'll snatch a picture and do it anyway.'

But Syd went a little too far and posed looking really glum so they had their story about him being forced back to his old trade of painting and decorating.

Syd and I have had our differences over the years but, as a double act, we always felt we had to defend each other. *I* can have a go at Syd if I feel like it, but I'll go mad if I hear anyone else criticising him. When I was ill as I got older, he would stick up for me. If people were rude, I would be rude back, instead of just smiling like I always used to, and Syd used to leap in and defend me. If you're not feeling too well it can be a little wearing to have fans coming up to pull your hair to see if it's real and saying, 'Oh you're fatter than I thought.'

But Syd can be very frustrating. Because of my health I couldn't work with him much in 2003 while Syd was in panto with Darren Day in Sunderland. Sitting at home alone, I watched the Rugby World Cup and came up with a Johnny Wilkinson gag for Syd. I rang him and told him to copy Johnny's famous arm movements and pretend to do a conversion with the mice when they changed into white horses. Next thing I knew, Syd was telling me that the gag worked a treat but he'd given it to Darren Day who was playing Buttons. I hit the roof. '*You're* my mate, not Darren Day,' I told him, but I'm not sure he got the point.

Even in the darkest days of my illness I used to say to Dave and Syd, 'Whatever happens, we've had a laugh. Apart from all the stress and illness, we have had a laugh.' They asked us to go on *The Weakest Link*, but as Syd didn't want to I did it on my own. It was OK. I think Anne Robinson frightens him, but then that's the whole point, and you know that if you do come back with some smart remark they would cut it out. Sometimes it is better to take a load of abuse. Sometimes it just goes with the territory. But Syd is a bit sensitive because he has been stitched up with a few of his decorating jobs by the papers. He is terrified they will say something about decorating.

Where Syd and I really differ is over religion. I'm not anti-religious. I was brought up as a Catholic, and my wife and other members of my family are very religious and I completely respect their views. But when it comes to the born-again showbusiness Christians it doesn't sit well with me because I doubt their motives. They don't seem to suddenly find their faith for any very positive reasons.

The born-agains in our business usually have a career that has gone belly-up, owe a load of money or, as in Syd's case, they have a guilt complex about something. And so they turn to religion. There are a lot of born-agains in prison with terrific guilt complexes about what they have done. Syd was on a guilt trip about Paul because he ignored his son all his life. Mavis deserves a medal for what she put up with trying to look after Paul. He was dreadful as a lad. I know how guilty Syd felt because he told me about it. He didn't know what school Paul went to or if he ever had a job. He just had absolutely nothing to do with his own son, no input into his life. It has always puzzled me. Can you be a born-again Christian on Tuesday and then change your mind again on Wednesday?

Syd is doing his own thing now. We still have niggles

but we know each other so well. It was always an unusual partnership in that we never sat down and said, 'Right, I'll do that and you do this.' We never rehearsed. We would just learn a song, out of the charts usually, and then go on and do it. Syd would be concentrating and trying to remember the chords on his guitar and I would be skylarking about. I had usually had a few pints just to give me some Dutch courage.

We'd come off and people would ask, 'How does your mate keep his face so straight?' I was never aware of that. I was just doing jokes that we used to do about Syd anyway. We always used to take the mickey out of him. Syd was like Eugene in *Grease* to his mates. Our act was based on real life: I'm a mickey taker and Syd is the sort of person who is often the butt of jokes. I wanted to be a singer, really, but the comedy came partly out of nerves. Other comics would watch us and give me lines like 'He's so thin he has to run round in the shower to get wet.' Or 'He's so thin he's playing the lead in *Lassie*.' If we ever attempted to do cross patter like traditional double acts, Syd would forget his lines and, being anxious, I would fill in for him.

Showbusiness certainly has its unpredictable moments. I was at a football match between Manchester City and Torquay and found myself talking to the former Manchester United manager Frank O'Farrell. He told me he was a prison visitor and one of the inmates was trying to compile a celebrity recipe book. Frank asked me to contribute and, even though my idea of *haute cuisine* is steak and chips, I wrote to this lad in Parkhurst.

Next thing I knew he had written back thanking me and asking me for a photograph for his friend Reg. It turned out to be Reg Kray, so I thought I'd better do as I was asked. Then I got a letter back saying this lad and Reg were writing a book on cockney rhyming slang and they wanted to get in touch with Dennis Waterman who was in *Minder* at the time. I sent them the address of Thames Television and left it at that.

Laughter remains very important to me, and one of the people who always brings it with him is Frank Carson. He's a naturally funny man. We met for a coffee recently at Gordano Services on the M5 as he was rushing up the motorway and he totally took over the place. The jokes might be familiar but then so are the smiles. If there were more people like Frank around, the world would be a happier place.

Norman Collier is another great friend who never fails to lift my spirits. I think he's perhaps the most naturally funny man I've ever met. And Norman and Frank together are a joy. We did three seasons together and every day we played golf together. We would play at ten with whoever was around.

One day, as we arrived at the first tee ,a young lad was just teeing off with his girlfriend caddying for him. Frank hurtled over. 'Young man, how'd you like to play with some stars? Come on, make up a four ball. What's your name?'

'Malcolm.'

'What do you play off?

'Six.'

'You play with me,' said Frank.

We set off, me and Norman against Frank and young Malcolm, but Frank wouldn't stop talking and the poor lad was so nervous he could hardly hit a ball. We won the first four holes and Frank turned to Malcolm who was only about 17. 'Are you on holiday, Malcolm?'

'Yes.'

'Well, next year make sure you go somewhere else.'

We all laughed, including Malcolm and his young girlfriend, because it wasn't meant unkindly. Even Tiger Woods couldn't play golf properly with Frank Carson rabbiting in his ear all the time.

We used to go in a Greek restaurant every night and, by the end, Norman had all the waiters doing comedy routines. He's irrepressible. On the last night, the waiters presented him with the top of a Belisha beacon and he just about brought the restaurant down with it.

People like Norman and Frank are priceless national treasures in my mind. They are both about 74 now and still going strong. Comedy is what keeps them going. You could add in Bernard Manning and Ken Dodd to that because they are both about the same age. They don't want to retire. What to? I still do my after-dinners and I try to do some charity work with my time.

Norman and Frank were just two of the guests when we were honoured with an appearance on *This Is Your Life* back in 1993. We were on stage sloshing around in the water, singing in the rain on stage at the Winter Gardens in Blackpool, when Michael Aspel surprised us. I was astonished and couldn't help but exclaim that we'd been waiting 30 years for this. It was fabulous to see all our family and friends. My sister Irene recalled me knocking together a homemade double bass and then singing Lonnie Donegan's 'Does Your Chewing Gum Lose Its Flavour' at a very early age. Jimmy Brown remembered my football prowess in remarkably glowing terms and Bernard Manning recorded his tribute. As he put it, 'All the good acts are working!' With two of my footballing heroes – Kevin Keegan and Mike Summerbee – there, it really was a great night.

Not everyone we knew was there, of course. Some people can never quite be trusted to tell the truth, even on *This Is Your Life*. Leslie Grantham is the biggest wind-up merchant of anyone I have ever met, so I didn't take all his internet nonsense too seriously. He came out to dinner with a mate of mine who was a bit starstruck and had asked if Leslie would come. Now these are normal people who are thrilled to be having dinner with Syd and Eddie and the guy who plays Dirty Den. We were all telling jokes and having a good time but Leslie started his wind-ups. He'd mention the name of a very famous actress and say, 'Did you know about her and the dogs?' And my friends were shocked. But, of course, he had to go too far.

I got a little tape recorder out of my bag and said, 'Grantham, I'm taping this and I'm going to sell it to the newspapers.' Just to stop him.

It's just his nature to wind people up all the time. That's his nature. When he heard Tony Booth was coming on to *EastEnders*, his first reaction was to ask, 'Has Pat Phoenix's money run out?' That's Leslie, straight in with both feet.

The great thing about my career is the number of laughs it has given me, and many of them have been on the golf course.

Bruce Forsyth is a fine player but you wouldn't have known that when he had a little trouble with the fans in a tournament we played in together. Bruce and I each walked forward to the tee. I was pretty nervous but I managed to hit the ball straight. Not that far, but straight. Loads of photographers moved forward as Bruce shaped to take his shot. They were in his line of sight. 'Do you mind, my love? Move back, one will get killed.' They were all laughing.

'Come on, my love, I'm trying to play golf here.'

They moved forward again and they were almost in front of him. Bruce was getting more and more annoyed. He had to hit it the third time but he'd just lost all concentration and he duffed it right through all these photographers. He started banging his club and saying, 'I can't play in these conditions.'

The crowd were crying with laughter but he wasn't being intentionally funny, he just didn't want to hit anyone and hurt them.

Seve Ballesteros is a much better golfer than me but he's still got a funny side. We were playing at St Mellion in Cornwall and a mate of mine was caddying for me. The team was going really well and Seve was great giving us advice and geeing us up. I was at the 17th. I don't know what county Seve was in but it wasn't Cornwall. Well, *he* was in Cornwall but his ball wasn't. I was on the edge of the green for two and I had a shot at this hole. I said to my mate, 'Give me my eight iron, I'm going to pitch and run it on to the green.'

Seve suddenly arrived at my shoulder. 'Eddie, you there for two?'

'Yes, Seve.'

'You on a shot?'

'Yes, Seve.'

'What do you play?'

'Eight iron, pitch and run,' which is a shot that pros don't play.

So he said, 'No, no, no. You use putter.'

'I'd rather use my eight.'

'No, no, no. You use putter.'

I wasn't too happy. I said to my mate who was caddying, 'He's never seen me hit my eight iron.'

'No, but he's Seve Ballesteros.'

I tried to explain and he said, 'Ah, you play what you want.'

After all this, I was settling down and in total turmoil. I went boom with my eight iron and I totally duffed it and hit it about two feet. It meant an extra stroke and we lost a hole we could have won. Afterwards, he made me play the shot with my putter.

He said, 'Hit the ball to the left of the hole.'

I did as I was told and the ball finished up about three inches from the hole.

I said, 'I'm sorry, Seve,' and he swore at me in Spanish.

The chance to meet your heroes and heroines is always well worth taking. I have fought all my life against shyness, but when we were at the London Palladium we were knocked out when Rita Moreno came up to us and introduced herself. She was the star of my all-time favourite musical *West Side Story* and she said, 'Hi, Little and Large, I'm Rita Moreno, nice to meet you.' I could hardly speak because she was so nice and down to earth.

Regrets? I suppose like anyone else I have a few. It's sad, but we never get repeated on TV. I think the audience is out there but I'm not a scheduler. We should get at least a *Best Of...*, even if the cynics would have it that it would only take ten minutes. We were lucky because we were on during perhaps the last period when families watched together. Nowadays, kids have a telly in their room, and DVD players, and there is so much more choice for everyone. I'm not saying it is a bad thing but it does tend to split up the family.

At the end, the only thing that saved us was the figures. The critics were merciless. If you're up, they like to knock you down and, when you're down, they like to give you a good kicking. We understood that but it was not pleasant. I once wrote to a journalist called Tony Pratt on the *Daily Mirror* who used to write the preview pages. He used to give us a good going over. I thought he was being unfair, so I wrote to him complaining that he seemed biased against us. Suddenly, he started giving us some great write-ups! We had audiences of up to 18 million people. Today, shows are a success if they can attract audiences of eight million.

CHAPTER TEN

Death And Life

I've cheated death four times in my life but I never really took my medical condition seriously until I realised I needed a heart transplant to save my life.

Over the years, I have kept countless medical warnings to myself and just soldiered on as best I could. I always thought I couldn't stop working. If I stopped working, Syd stopped working and I thought we might never start again. If I am honest, and I am certainly trying to be now, my health has been a problem many times before. In Blackpool in 1977, I went on stage with a temperature of 103 when I had peritonitis. But I know that Syd has gone on stage with high temperatures as well. I've seen him coughing and spluttering through the act. In a double act, you have a responsibility to each other.

The heart problems began in earnest in 1991 when I blacked out at home. The doctor diagnosed an irregular heartbeat and I was fitted with a pacemaker. I thought I was fine. I just carried on as normal doing summer season cabarets. The pacemaker just regulates your heart, but I thought I could carry on as normal and over the years its condition continued to deteriorate.

In 1993, my heart was attacked by a virus and I suffered from heart failure. I learned later that I could have dropped dead at any moment after that. But I belong to the old school of showbusiness which decrees that the show must go on whatever. I ignored countless twinges and even carried on through a mild stroke back in 1996.

I fell ill in Newcastle and went to see a really bolshie heart woman who my doctor had told me visit. She said, 'The only thing that will help you is a heart transplant.' It was the first time it had been mentioned. I went back to the flat and told Patsy. It was a terrible time. I couldn't sleep. I was struggling to get through the act but I didn't want anybody else to know about it. It was horrendous and just Patsy and myself knew.

I tried to carry on but my health gradually got worse. In 2001, the doctor said, 'You have just got to stop working now.' But doctors don't know the nature of showbusiness. He advised me to just work occasional days all carefully planned out to give maximum rest in between. It doesn't work like that. You can get a call telling you to do something at the other end of the country next week, and if you want to work you do it. That's the nature of the business.

I was warned to stop and I ignored the warning. I was an idiot, I suppose, but I worried, if I stopped working, who was going to pay the bills? I was still paying big maintenance payments to my ex-wife.

You could hardly get a harsher schedule than the one we were working at the time. We were doing Monday night in Scarborough, Tuesday night in Filey, Wednesday night in Mablethorpe, and the next night in Skegness and two nights in Yarmouth. We worked six nights along the east coast and then had one day off. The next six nights would be on the west coast, then it would be Cornwall, and so on. It was a dreadfully punishing schedule if you were fit. But I was fit to drop.

Derek would laugh at me because I found it difficult to walk a few yards to get the papers. Slight inclines used to make me collapse. Holiday camps were a hard audience. I shouldn't have been working at all but I kept going and tried to disguise from my wife how bad I felt. It was stupid but being half of Little and Large is not like a normal career.

By the time Syd and I appeared in *Babes In The Wood* in Hull in December 2001, I knew I was desperately ill. Syd admits now that he should have stopped me from going on, but to be fair to him I should have stopped myself. I was in a terrible state. My heart was so weak that it wasn't pumping blood round properly. I was only drinking water and I wasn't eating at all yet I was getting bigger and bigger.

I found myself sitting exhausted on a bench by the side of the stage. The stage manager would bring me a glass of water and I couldn't get up. Syd would say, 'Come on,' but I couldn't. It was absolutely pathetic. He'd say, 'It's only ten minutes,' but I could hardly manage. We even had a dance routine which I'd somehow struggle through and then come off and simply collapse.

I was so fat I couldn't put my seatbelt on. I was so ill I used to get the car to get as close as possible to the door of the hotel. The effort of walking was unbearable. At home, I used the stair lift we had put in for my mother-in-law. I couldn't sleep properly at night: if I lay down for too long my lungs, filled up with water so I used to get up every night and sit watching television.

I was on Warfarin tablets to thin my blood and I had to have my INR checked regularly to make sure my blood count stayed with the limits. If it gets too thin, you could cut yourself shaving and bleed to death, which almost happened to me.

I was trying to get my INR done but I kept putting it off as you do in showbiz. The panto finishes in ten days, let's leave it until then, was my attitude. When I got back, I went straight to the doctor to have my INR done. He phoned me up very worried because it was sky high. He said, 'Stop the Warfarin tonight and come in for another INR test tomorrow.' I did that and he was horrified. 'Eddie,' he said, 'it is higher than it was yesterday. What's going on? You're carrying an awful lot of liquid, you're going to have to go in hospital to get yourself sorted out.'

I went up to 17 stone. I was like a balloon full of water. I went into Southmead Hospital and they put me on water tablets. I lost seven pounds the first night and seven pounds the second night, all of it liquid. In ten days, I lost two stone. They sent me home and increased my water tablets and restricted my liquid intake. Then it went the other way and I started to dry out. I started feeling dizzy, which is when I got up to pee and fainted, falling through these little doors in the bathroom. I tried to pretend to Patsy that I just tripped in the dark. I lied that I didn't want to put the light on and wake her. But really I was lying to myself.

I had to go to a golf club to present some prizes. I did it, but on the Monday I had to go back to the hospital as an outpatient for a check-up. They told me to lie on the bed and I fainted. My kidneys were failing now. The next minute I was in intensive care with no idea what was wrong with me and Patsy was by the bedside desperately worried. No one was telling me anything.

Patsy said they were trying to get an air ambulance and, even though I was a bit out of it, that sounded quite serious. I might not be very medically aware but I know you don't have an air ambulance for an in-growing toenail. In the end, they decided to send me in an ambulance, with Patsy following in a cab. The parting words from the doctor to Patsy before we went were: 'Your husband might not survive the journey.'

I didn't know this, of course, but I had a doctor and a nurse with me in the ambulance. They put a line in a main vein in my neck and all different-coloured leads that they were going to connect up when we got to Papworth. Everyone seemed a bit tense except for me so as usual I tried to joke my way out of the problem. No one had really told me that I was ill. I knew I was ill but, while I didn't feel great, I didn't feel as if I was at death's door. You know what comics are like, we make stories out of everything.

Patsy had phoned my daughters and they were driving to Papworth Hospital. They had picked up my son Ryan from university in Manchester and turned the radio on to hear the headline 'Comedy legend dies'. That upset them, but tragically it was Spike Milligan they were talking about. I'm pretty sure that, even in my wildest dreams, I don't qualify as a comedy legend but it was still enough to scare my kids.

When we got to Papworth, I was in a sort of daze, and lying in bed I became convinced that I was dreaming it all. About seven doctors came in and they stood around my bed. They all seemed to be from different races, and this was when, in my addled state, I thought I had become the latest star of the new James Bond film and this was just an elaborate scene with all the baddies lined up to do their worst. I was hooked up to all the drugs by then so I really was not myself.

Suddenly the tall blonde one said, 'Velcome to Papworth, Mr McGinnis.'

I was close to death but, thankfully, I was in just the right place. They got my kidneys back to normal in a few days. The liquid left my body so comprehensively that one of the transplant consultants, a laconic chap called Michael Woods, observed, 'Eddie, you're so dry you're a fire risk.'

It was the professionalism of the medical staff that is my lasting memory. There is a brilliant consultant transplant cardiologist at Papworth called Mr Jayan Parameshwar who gave me a real telling-off for not losing enough weight. I was close to tears. Very much later I said to him, 'When I left Bristol, I was seriously ill but you didn't seem all that concerned or worried.'

He said, 'Someone else's seriously ill is not our seriously ill.'

That first night I spent in hospital was also memorable to me for another reason. Manchester City were playing Sheffield Wednesday. I was in intensive care with a nurse on duty near my bed all night. I said to Ryan, 'Whatever time it is, please ring me and tell me the score.' There was no Teletext in the hotel where they were staying and so I told Ryan, 'Phone up your uncle Brian and ask him how City have gone on.'

It got to about 10.15 and the match had been over for at least half an hour so I was really on edge. I rang my sister, Irene, who was alarmed to hear from me because Patsy had told her that I was at death's door. I said I was all right now and advised them against coming all the way down to visit me. I said, 'Have you got Teletext on your telly?'

She didn't know but her husband Harry assured her they did. When I asked them to look up to see the Manchester City result they were definitely not impressed. 'Edward,' said my sister. 'If you had died tonight and gone to the Pearly Gates, is the first thing you'd have said, "How's City gone on?"'

I couldn't argue. I think it probably would have been exactly that.

My most memorable conversation was with a surgeon who was coincidentally called Stephen Large. He said, 'Right, Eddie, I'm Stephen Large.'

I said, 'Are you taking the mickey?'

He said, 'No, it's no joke.' And he explained he had been considering giving me a mechanical heart, but they had rejected that alternative and decided I had to have a full-blown transplant. He told me I had to lose a load of weight before they could operate.

I said, 'Mr Large, you can't be serious. We share a common name.'

He said, 'Listen, you. When you and that pal of yours were on telly in the 1970s and 1980s, my life was a bloody misery. You're losing the weight.'

He was desperate to do the operation but he didn't do it in the end. It was a pity. I was thinking of the publicity: 'Large has Large in stitches'. But the weight, fortunately, was mainly water.

With hindsight, I regret keeping it from Patsy so much. She has been my strength, she's got me through it. The rush to Papworth happened in 2002. I had to lose the weight and I was put on the list for a heart transplant in March 2003, once the weight was gone, and I got the new heart in June. I was lucky really.

We had one false alarm that was another drama. Ryan was going back to university in Manchester so we were driving him up. I had a bleeper from the hospital that they give you when you're on the transplant list, but I'd not had a call. At first I was frightened even to go for a pee in case they called but you relax after a few days.

I'd had it six or eight weeks and we were just on the M6 north of Birmingham when, of course, it rang. 'Eddie, this is Michael from Papworth. Are you driving? Yes. Well, pull over and ring me back.'

'Is it a go?'

'I don't want to saying anything when you're driving.'

So I did as I was told. I saw my wife and son start to show a little bit of emotion but I was really excited. I pulled into Hilton Park Services and had the conversation I'd been waiting for. They sent the ambulance to Ryan's place in Manchester. I got to Papworth about five and hit them with a flurry of jokes as usual. I was full of beans and when Patsy arrived I said, 'I'm going to be a new man, aren't I?' On the outside it's the comedian speaking and relentlessly clowning around, but on the inside little Eddie

McGinnis from Glasgow is absolutely shitting himself. I had never been so scared in my life.

At a quarter to seven, Michael walked in and said, 'The operation is off. The heart isn't good enough. The left ventricle is slightly stretched.' At a pinch, they might have done it but this is how careful they are. We just had to go back home and begin waiting all over again. On the way to the hospital I'd rung my daughters, several mates, including Kevin Keegan, the Manchester City manager, to give him some team advice he definitely didn't need or listen to probably, but I was on a sort of high. Now I had to come down to earth and I even managed to make jokes about having had it done and being on my way back to the golf course. Inside, I was very disappointed, but I didn't want anyone to see that so I used the jokes again.

Then we went up to Manchester again to bring Ryan back for the summer holidays. As soon as he got back, he went out with his mates and the call came again. An ambulance arrived an hour and a half later. They were very confident. I went out to tell Patsy and suddenly I cracked up and found myself crying. I said, 'That was Papworth.'

At first she thought I was joking, until she saw the tears. Our good friends Jean and John Mays stepped in to take care of Patsy's mum and off we went.

The second time, my mind was better prepared. I was in the ambulance and I said to the paramedic, 'I hope this isn't a false alarm. I've had one of those already. I can't go through that again.'

He said, 'Eddie, there's a bloke near you who's had seven false alarms.'

'You're joking.'

'No, he lives the other side of Bristol and he's been taken in seven times and gone home each time without the op.' I met him later when I got to the hospital and he was eighth time lucky.

I was operated on at three in the morning. It was a six-hour operation but, of course, you have no concept of what is going on. Days later, I asked Patsy what she and Ryan had done. 'We just sat outside all night,' she said.

I was a terrible patient. When I came round, all I wanted to do was moan, going on about the pain. I still had the dressing from a kidney operation four days before (my kidneys had started to fail again and, ironically, you have to be pretty fit to have a heart transplant). They got me back to health and four days later I had the operation. I was still out of it and at first confused the two ops, not even realising I'd had the big one. I must have asked about 50 times why I was in such pain.

When I had the kidney failure, the doctor said, 'Look, you're seriously ill, you must not work.'

So I had to phone up Syd and break it to him that I couldn't work. We weren't getting a lot of work at the time anyway, although I did do a couple of lunch speeches while all this was going on.

After the operation, I did not feel instantly better. It was weird, I was sort of in denial. What has been great for me is that people have said how much better I look. It's just so great to be able to walk round and live a normal life without getting hopelessly out of breath. When I first came home, I went a bit mad and I was going to the gym five times a week. But that was overdoing it and I've cut back a bit: I'm in my sixties now.

We spent a month at Papworth, by which time the road tax had run out on the car. On the way to pay it in a village near Papworth, I had fallen over because I was so weak I couldn't even climb a pavement. I clipped the kerb and fell, and my arms were too weak to take the weight of my body and smashed my glasses and cut all my face. I had to have tetanus injections and everything.

Eventually, when I did get to the Post Office, I said, 'I would have been in sooner but I had a change of heart.' I thought here we go again.

Jokes helped me through my transplant. Bobby Davro threatened to come and disguise himself in a doctor's coat but I'm pleased he didn't because he'd probably have caused mayhem. He's a lively lad. One of the first to phone up was Bob Monkhouse, but I didn't recognise his voice, and Bradley Walsh from *Coronation Street*, who's a pal, was on the phone as well.

At one point, Bernard Manning phoned me. It shows how the image of people affects others, as the nurse was holding the phone at arm's length as she brought Bernard to me. But he's a nice bloke. He knew exactly what to say to a comic in hospital: 'Now you can work on your ****ing act.' Not, 'How are you?' or anything like that. Showbusiness helps you to cope. Tarbuck rang me and slagged me off instead of asking me how I was. He was doing gags about me. No sympathy at all which is what I want of course.

Syd was supportive throughout the heart transplant but, afterwards, I came to realise it was very unlikely that we would ever work together again. What really came between us was much more recent though.

We were offered a tour in October 2003, five months after my operation. It was for six weeks from March 2004 and it was going to be Cannon and Ball, Little and Large, Ray Alan and Lord Charles, and two of the Grumbleweeds – Graham and Robin – a tour of double acts. I was keen to get back to work. Syd phoned me up about the tour sounding very unenthusiastic.

He said, 'Oh, have you seen the dates?'

'No,' I replied.

'It looks very hard work,' said Syd. 'I'm not sure you're going to be up to it. It might be too much for you after your operation.'

A few weeks went by and I got the details of the tour dates. Again, Syd said, 'I don't think you'll be able to do all these dates. It's a very tough schedule.'

I thought I could manage and I said so.

Next day, he rang again: 'Are we all supposed to be on the same money for this tour?'

I agreed that was the deal.

'Well,' Syd said, 'I was round at Bobby Ball's house and he let it slip that they are getting a lot more money than anyone else. That's not right, is it?'

I tried to stay non-committal, but it didn't take a genius to work out that Syd didn't want to do the tour. We had yet another conversation and Syd was moaning on about what a tough tour it was and I said, 'You don't want to do this tour, do you?'

He said, 'No, not really.'

So as usual I had to be the front man again and do the difficult bit, phoning up and using my health to pull out of the tour. Syd didn't want to do it and we had to make some excuse so the tour was cancelled.

A week or two after the tour was cancelled, Syd phoned up and said, 'Could I go on the tour on my own?'

It was quite obvious to me then that our partnership was over. It is fair enough if he doesn't want to work with me any more. I had been ill for a while and he had started to work on his own. I can see his point of view. I don't bear any grudges about it but I do wish he had told me to my face. But that is what I had to put up with for 40 years.

The truth has always been a moving target to Syd. If you saw him tomorrow and asked him why we didn't do that tour, he would say, 'Oh, Eddie couldn't do it.' Syd finds it impossible to take the blame or responsibility for anything.

I'm not unhappy about not working together any more, to be honest. We weren't getting much work anyway;

when the big clubs started to close, we struggled for work. The reason we had left Norman Murray in 1985 was because we were not getting enough work. When I was told not to work, we only had three dates in the diary, so it's not as if me being ill put us out of work. We were already out of work.

I don't know whose heart I was given, but I got a Christmas card from the donor's wife. Contact between the families of heart donors and recipients is a very difficult area and Papworth try to handle it as sensitively as possible. You're encouraged to send an anonymous message to the family of the person whose heart you have been given.

I think it was the hardest letter I have ever had to write in my life. I tried to spell out the enormous benefits the heart had given me, how I was living long enough to see my grandchildren and so on. But I was very aware that in saying how fantastic I felt there was a danger of upsetting them. It was a fine balance and took me a long time to write.

I explained that all my grandchildren saw before the operation was an old man sitting permanently out of breath. But now, thanks to them, I am able to go out in the garden and play with my grandchildren. I said I think about the donor and his precious gift every day, which I genuinely do. I just wanted to give them what comfort I could that their amazing generosity and warmth of spirit had not gone unrecognised.

There have been experiments in America where donor families have been put in touch with recipients and sometimes it can be upsetting. Although the recipients are incredibly grateful, there are only so many times they can say thank you to the donor's family for saving their lives. Sometimes they became friends but later resentment set in because the family who had suffered the loss found it hard to deal with. So the experiment was abandoned.

If I pushed it, I could find out the identity of my heart donor but I'm not sure if I want to. After I had written, I received a Christmas card from the donor's family hoping I was well, but not giving any name or address. It was very nice, so perhaps it is best left like that. I know people who have gone to great lengths to contact their donors and I'm not sure that's quite right. One lad even asked his donor's family if the person whose heart he had used to like curry. It seems he had developed a taste for curry after his operation! I believe that whoever decided to let me have his heart was a wonderful person and I wouldn't like to do anything to cause pain or discomfort for any member of his family.

I just joke that I hope he wasn't a Manchester United fan, because if he was I'd have to have it taken out!